CONTEMPORARY SOCIAL ISSUES: A BIBLIOGRAPHIC SERIES

No. 19

RAPE: A BIBLIOGRAPHY

compiled by Joan Nordquist

Reference and Research Services

RAPE: A BIBLIOGRAPHY

ISBN 0-937855-36-7

Contemporary Social Issues: A Bibliographic Series, No. 19

ISSN 0887-3569

Published in 1990 by
Reference and Research Services
511 Lincoln Street
Santa Cruz, CA 95060 USA

Contemporary Social Issues: A Bibliographic Series will issue four bibliographies a year. Subscriptions are $45/year, standing orders $15 each bibliography, individual bibliographies are $15 each.

TABLE OF CONTENTS

Introduction to the Series

CONTEMPORARY SOCIAL ISSUES: A BIBLIOGRAPHIC SERIES

Library users have an avid interest and continuing need for the most up-to-date and accurate information on a variety of contemporary social issues. Therefore, a new bibliographic series on contemporary social issues which will cover current topics such as investment and social responsibility, comparable worth, university research: social and political implications, and domestic violence is a truly worth while reference source.

These bibliographies are not simply one long list of books and journals on the subject but entries are arranged under useful categories. Included are useful and hard-to-find directories, bibliographies, activist organizations, and periodicals on the topic. Authoritative books, pamphlets, documents and periodical articles are cited representing a variety of viewpoints and ranging from general to scholarly works.

It would take endless hours for a library user to gather together all this information in one spot, so it is indeed a pleasure to have it all in one well-thought-out and current ready reference source. **Contemporary Social Issues: A Bibliographic Series** should be made readily available in all libraries to be used by librarians and library users.

Jacquelyn Marie
Reference Librarian
University of California, Santa Cruz

RAPE: A BIBLIOGRAPHY

The bibliography is divided into ten main sections.

SECTION 1. contains works about the occurence of rape in our society. Material about child sexual abuse is not included in this bibliography. The citations in this section are divided into five sections: (1) GENERAL WORKS, (2) HISTORY, (3) MARITAL RAPE, (4) DATE AND ACQUAINTANCE RAPE, and (5) MALE RAPE.

SECTION 2. provides material on the psychological impact of rape on the victim. **SECTION 3.** lists books, pamphlets and articles about the treatment and services for rape victims. **SECTION 4.** contains works examining attitudes about rape in our society. **SECTION 5.** provides information about race and class issues. **SECTION 6.** provides research discussing the psychological and sociological profile of rapists. **SECTION 7.** lists books and research articles about the effect of pornography on sexual violence. **SECTION 8.** provides information about the prevention of rape. **SECTION 9.** contains material on the legal aspects. **SECTION 10.** gives resources: (1) STATISTICS, (2) BIBLIOGRAPHIES, (3) DIRECTORIES, and (4) ORGANIZATIONS.

The entries in Sections 1 - 9 are divided by format into (1) books, pamphlets, papers, documents, and (2) articles in periodicals and books.

The entries are arranged alphabetically by author or title (in the case of a corporate author). The sources selected for inclusion in the bibliography represent the various viewpoints on the topic. Works from the psychological, social, feminist and legal literature are included. The entries, particularly the periodical literature, generally date from the last five years.

BOOKS, DOCUMENTS, PAMPHLETS

Adler, Zsuzsanna. Rape on Trial. New York: Routledge and Kegan Paul, 1987

Ageton, Suzanne. Sexual Assault among Adolescents. Lexington, MA: Lexington Books, 1983

Baron, Larry and Straus, Murray. Four Theories of Rape in American Society: A State-Level Analysis. New Haven: Yale University Press, 1989

Beneke, Timothy. Men on Rape. New York: St. Martin's Press, 1982

Benn, Melissa and others. The Rape Controversy. London: NCCL Rights for Women Unit, 1986 32p

Booher, Dianna. Rape: What Would You Do If---?. New York: J. Messner, 1981

Botkin-Maher, Jennifer. Nice Girls Don't Get Raped. San Bernadino, CA: Here's Life Publishers, 1987

Bourque, Linda. Defining Rape. Durham: Duke University Press, 1989

Box, Steven. Power, Crime, and Mystification. New York: Tavistock Publications, 1983

Boyle, Christine. Sexual Assault. Toronto, Canada: Carswell, 1984

Brownmiller, Susan. Against Our Will. New York: Simon and Schuster, 1975

Burgess, Ann, ed. Rape and Sexual Assault: A Resource Handbook. New York: Garland Publishing, 1985

_____. Rape and Sexual Assault II. New York: Garland Publishing, 1988

Cann, Arnie and others. Rape. Ann Arbor, MI: Society for the Psychological Study of Social Issues, 1981

Dean, Charles and deBruyn-Kops, Mary. The Crime and the Consequences of Rape. Springfield, IL: Thomas, 1982

Ellis, Lee. Theories of Rape: Inquiries into the Causes of Sexual Aggression. New York: Hemisphere Publishing Corporation, 1989

Esper, Jody and Runge, Christopher. The Long-Term Effects of Rape on Lifestyle and Psychological Functioning. 1988 26p (Paper presented at the American Psychological Association, 1988) (available from ERIC, No.ED304593)

Estrich, Susan. Real Rape. Cambridge, MA: Harvard University Press, 1987

Fortune, Marie. Sexual Violence: The Unmentionable Sin. New York: Pilgrim Press, 1983

Goldstein, Carol. The Dilemma of the Rape Victim: A Descriptive Analysis. Huntsville, TX: Institute of Contemporary Corrections and the Behavioral Sciences, Sam Houston State University, 1976 26p

Gordon, Margaret and Riger, Stephanie. The Female Fear. New York: Free Press, 1989

Green, William. The Evidential Examination and Management of the Adult Female Victim. Lexington, MA: Lexington Books, 1988

Griffin, Susan. Rape, the Politics of Consciousness. San Francisco: Harper and Row, 1986

Gunn, Rita. Sexual Assault: The Dilemma of Disclosure, the Question of Conviction. Winnipeg: University of Manitoba Press, 1988

Hopkins, June, ed. Perspectives on Rape and Sexual Assault. London: Harper and Row, 1984

Horos, Carol. Rape. New Canaan, CT: Tobey, 1974

Johnson, Kathryn. If You Are Raped: What Every Woman Needs to Know. Holmes Beach, FL: Learning Publications, 1985

Kelly, Liz. Surviving Sexual Violence. Minneapolis, MN: University of Minnesota Press, 1989

McEvoy, Alan and Brookings, Jeff. If She Is Raped: A Book for Husbands, Fathers, and Male Friends. Holmes Beach, FL: Learning Publications, 1984

Price, Lisa. In Women's Interests: Feminist Activism and Institutional Change. Vancouver: Women's Research Centre, 1988 56p

Qureshi, Donna. Rape: Social Facts from England and America. Champaign, IL: Stipes Publishing, 1979

Roberts, Cathy. Women and Rape. New York: New York University Press, 1989

Rowland, Judith. The Ultimate Violation. Garden City, NY: Doubleday, 1985

Russell, Diana. The Politics of Rape: The Victim's Perspective. New York: Stein and Day, 1984

_____. Sexual Exploitation: Rape, Child Sexual Abuse and Workplace Harrassment. Beverly Hills, CA: Sage, 1984

Sexual Violence, the Reality for Women. London: Women's Press, 1984

Stanko, Elizabeth. Everyday Violence: How Women and Men Experience Sexual and Physical Danger. Winchester, MA: Pandora Press, 1990

Sunday, Suzanne and Fobach, Ethel, eds. Violence Against Women: A Critique of the Socio-Biology Rape. New York: Grodian Press, 1985

Te Paske, Bradley. Rape and Ritual: A Psychological Study. Toronto, Canada: Inner City Books, 1982

Tomaselli, Sylvana and Porter, Ray, eds. Rape. New York: Blackwell, 1986

Toner, Barbara. The Facts of Rape. London: Arrow Books, 1982

United States. Congress. Senate. Committee on the Judiciary. Juvenile Rape Victims, Hearing. Washington, DC: Government Printing Office, 1985 43p

United States. Department of Health and Human Services. National Institute of Mental Health. National Center for the Prevention and Control of Rape. The Sexual Victimization of Adolescents. Washington, DC: Government Printing Office, 1985 48p

RAPE
GENERAL

ARTICLES

Abarbanel, Gail. "Rape and Resistance", JOURNAL OF INTERPERSONAL VIOLENCE 1(1):100-105 1986

Baber, H. "How Bad Is Rape?", HYPATIA 2(2):125-138 1987

Ball, Christine. "Women, Rape and War: Patriarchal Functions and Ideologies", ATLANTIS 12(1):83-91 1986

Barnett, M. and others. "Similarity and Empathy: The Experience of Rape", JOURNAL OF SOCIAL PSYCHOLOGY 126:47-49 February 1986

Baron, Larry. "Does Rape Contribute to Reproductive Success? Evaluation of Sociobiological Views of Rape", INTERNATIONAL JOURNAL OF WOMEN'S STUDIES 8:266-277 May/June 1985

_____ and Straus, Murray. "Four Theories of Rape: A Macrosociological Analysis", SOCIAL PROBLEMS 34(5):467-489 December 1987

_____ and others. "Sexual Assault in a College Community", SOCIOLOGICAL FOCUS 19(1):1-26 January 1986

Bart, Pauline. "A Study of Women Who Both Were Raped and Avoided Rape", JOURNAL OF SOCIAL ISSUES 37(4):123-137 1981

Bauermeister, Martin. "Rapists, Victims and Society", INTERNATIONAL JOURNAL OF OFFENDER THERAPY AND COMPARATIVE CRIMINOLOGY 21(3):238-248 1977

Berger, V. "Not So Simple Rape", CRIMINAL JUSTICE ETHICS 7:69-81 Winter/Spring 1988

Caringella-MacDonald, Susan. "Parallels and Pitfalls: The Aftermath of Legal Reform for Sexual Assault, Marital Rape, and Domestic Violence Victims", JOURNAL OF INTERPERSONAL VIOLENCE 3(2):174-189 June 1988

Cartwright, P. and Moore, R. "The Elderly Victim of Rape", SOUTHERN MEDICAL JOURNAL 82(8):988-989 August 1989

Chancer, Lynn. "New Bedford, Massachusetts, March 6, 1983-March 22, 1984: The 'Before and After' of a Group Rape", GENDER AND SOCIETY 1(3):239-260 September 1987

Check, James and Malamuth, Neil. "An Empirical Assessment of Some Feminist Hypotheses about Rape", INTERNATIONAL JOURNAL OF WOMEN'S STUDIES 8(4):414-423 1985

Christopher, F. "An Initial Investigation into a Continuum of Premarital Sexual Pressure", JOURNAL OF SEX RESEARCH 25:255-266 May 1988

9

DiVasto, Peter and others. "The Prevalence of Sexually Stressful Events among Females in the General Population", ARCHIVES OF SEXUAL BEHAVIOR 13(1):59-67 February 1984

Donnerstein, E. and Linz, D. "Sexual Violence in the Media: A Warning", PSYCHOLOGY TODAY 18:14-15 January 1984

Ellis, Lee and Beattie, Charles. "The Feminist Explanation of Rape: An Empirical Test", JOURNAL OF SEX RESEARCH 19(1):74-93 February 1983

Ellis, Megan. "Re-Defining Rape: Re-Victimizing Women", RESOURCES FOR FEMINIST RESEARCH 3:96-99 September 1988

Feldman-Summers, Shirley and Ashworth, Clark. "Factors Related to Intentions to Report a Rape", JOURNAL OF SOCIAL ISSUES 37(4):53-70 1981

Ferraro, Kathleen. "Opening Closing Doors", CONTEMPORARY SOCIOLOGY 15(1):50-52 January 1986

Franks, David. "Role-Taking, Social Power and Imperceptiveness: The Analysis of Rape", STUDIES IN SYMBOLIC INTERACTION 6:229-259 1985

Galvin, J. and Ladouceur, P., eds. "Rape [Symposium]", CRIME AND DELINQUENCY 31:163-331 April 1985

Giacopassi, David and Wilkinson, Karen. "Rape and the Devalued Victim", LAW AND HUMAN BEHAVIOR 9(4):367-383 December 1985

Gibbons, Donald. "Forcible Rape and Sexual Violence", JOURNAL OF RESEARCH IN CRIME AND DELINQUENCY 21(3):251-269 August 1984

Gray, Michael and others. "Sexual Aggression and Victimization: A Local Perspective", RESPONSE TO THE VICTIMIZATION OF WOMEN AND CHILDREN 11(3):9-13 1988

Gunn, Rita and Minch, Candice. "Unofficial and Official Responses to Sexual Assault", RESOURCES FOR FEMINIST RESEARCH 14:47-49 December 1985/January 1986

Hall, Eleanor and Flannery, Patricia. "Prevalence and Correlates of Sexual Assault Experiences in Adolescents", VICTIMOLOGY 9(3/4):398-406 1984

Heise, Lori. "International Dimensions of Violence Against Women", RESPONSE TO THE VICTIMIZATION OF WOMEN AND CHILDREN 12(1):3-11 1989

Holmstrom, Lynda and Burgess, Ann. "Rape and Everyday Life", SOCIETY 5(145):33-40 July/Aug 1983

Humphries, Drew. "Murdered Mothers, Missing Wives: Reconsidering Female Victimization", SOCIAL JUSTICE 17(2):71-89 Summer 1990

Kanekar, S. and others. "Causal and Moral Responsibility of Victims of Rape and Robbery", JOURNAL OF APPLIED SOCIAL PSYCHOLOGY 15(7):622-637 1985

Koss, Mary and others. "The Scope of Rape: Incidence and Prevalence of Sexual Aggression and Victimization in a National Sample of Higher Education Students", JOURNAL OF CONSULTING AND CLINICAL PSYCHOLOGY 55(2):162-170 April 1987

10

Kruttschnitt, C. "A Sociological, Offender-Based, Study of Rape", SOCIOLOGICAL QUARTERLY 30(2):305-329 Summer 1989

Lawson, J. and Hillix, W. "Coercion and Seduction in Robbery and Rape", PSYCHOLOGY TODAY 19:50-53 February 1985

Lizotte, Alan. "The Uniqueness of Rape: Reporting Assaultive Violence to the Police", CRIME AND DELINQUENCY 31(2):169-190 April 1985

Marshall, W. and Barbaree, H. "A Behavioral View of Rape", INTERNATIONAL JOURNAL OF LAW AND PSYCHIATRY 7(1):51-77 1984

McPherson, Heather. "The Apple Belonged to Eve: Rape, Incest and Re-Telling Myths", WOMEN'S STUDIES JOURNAL 3:22-28 March 1987

Michael, R. and Zumpe, D. "Sexual Violence in the United States and the Role of Season", AMERICAN JOURNAL OF PSYCHIATRY 140:883-886 July 1983
Discussion. AMERICAN JOURNAL OF PSYCHIATRY 141:1015-1016 August 1984
Discussion. AMERICAN JOURNAL OF PSYCHIATRY 141:1133 September 1984

Nicarthy, Ginny. "From the Sounds of Silence to the Roar of a Global Movement: Notes on the Movement Against Violence Against Women", RESPONSE TO THE VICTIMIZATION OF WOMEN AND CHILDREN 12(2):3-10 1989

Palmer, Craig. "Is Rape A Cultural Universal? A Re-Examination of the Ethnographic Data", ETHNOLOGY 28(1):1-16 January 1989
_____. "Rape in Nonhuman Animal Species: Definitions, Evidence, and Implications", JOURNAL OF SEX RESEARCH 26:355-374 August 1989
_____. "Twelve Reasons Why Rape Is Not Sexually Motivated: A Skeptical Examination", JOURNAL OF SEX RESEARCH 25:512-530 November 1988

Pitch, Tamar. "Critical Criminology, the Construction of Social Problems and the Question of Rape", INTERNATIONAL JOURNAL OF THE SOCIOLOGY OF LAW 13(1):25-46 February 1985

Ploughman, Penelope and Stensrud, John. "The Ecology of Rape Victimization: A Case Study of Buffalo, New York", GENETIC, SOCIAL, AND GENERAL PSYCHOLOGY MONOGRAPHS 112(3):303-324 August 1986

Poppen, P. and Segal, N. "The Influence of Sex and Sex Role Orientation on Sexual Coercion", SEX ROLES 19:689-701 December 1988

Renner, K. and others. "The 'Social' Nature of Sexual Assault", CANADIAN PSYCHOLOGY 29(2):163-173 April 1988

Reynolds, Lynn. "Rape: A Social Perspective", JOURNAL OF OFFENDER COUNSELING, SERVICES AND REHABILITATION 9(1/2):149-160 Fall/Winter 1984

Rivera, G. and Regoli, R. "Sexual Victimization Experiences of Sorority Women", SOCIOLOGY AND SOCIAL RESEARCH 72:39-42 October 1987

11

Roark, Mary. "Sexual Violence", NEW DIRECTIONS FOR STUDENT SERVICES 47:41-52 1989

Russell, Diana. "The Incest Legacy: Why Today's Abused Children Become Tomorrow's Victims of Rape", SCIENCES 26(2):28-32 March/April 1986

Schneider, Susan. "Why Jewish Women Get Raped", LILITH 15:8-12 Summer 1986

Silverman, Daniel and others. "Blitz Rape and Confidence Rape: A Typology Applied to 1,000 Consecutive Cases", AMERICAN JOURNAL OF PSYCHIATRY 145(11):1438-1441 November 1988

Steketee, G. and Austin, A. "Rape Victims and the Justice System -- Utilization and Impact", SOCIAL SERVICE SYSTEM 63(2):285-303 June 1989

Thornhill, Randy and Thornhill, Nancy. "Human Rape: An Evolutionary Analysis", ETHOLOGY AND SOCIOBIOLOGY 4(3):137-173 1983

Towson, S. and Zanna, M. "Retaliation Against Sexual Assault: Self-Defense or Public Duty?", PSYCHOLOGY OF WOMEN QUARTERLY 8:89-99 Fall 1983

Valentich, Mary and Gripton, James. "Ideological Perspectives on the Sexual Assault of Women", SOCIAL SERVICE REVIEW 58(3):448-461 September 1984

"Violent Crime [Reports of the National Center for the Analysis of Violent Crime]", FBI LAW ENFORCEMENT BULLETIN 54:1-31 August 1985

Walsh, A. "The Sexual Stratification Hypothesis and Sexual Assault in Light of the Changing Conceptions of Race", CRIMINOLOGY 25:153-173 February 1987

Warr, Mark. "Fear of Rape among Urban Women", SOCIAL PROBLEMS 32(3):238-250 February 1985

_____. "Rape, Burglary, and Opportunity", JOURNAL OF QUANTITATIVE CRIMINOLOGY 4(3):275-288 September 1988

Williams, Linda. "The Classic Rape: When Do Victims Report?", SOCIAL PROBLEMS 31(4):459-467 April 1984

Wilson, W. "Rape as Entertainment", PSYCHOLOGICAL REPORTS 63:607-610 October 1988

BOOKS

Carter, John. Rape in Medieval England: An Historical and Sociological Study. Lanham, MD: University Press of America, 1985

Clark, Anna. Women's Silence, Men's Violence: Sexual Assault in England, 1770-1845. New York: Pandora, 1987

Pleck, Elizabeth. Domestic Tyranny: The Making of American Social Policy Against Family Violence from Colonial Times to the Present. New York: Oxford University Press, 1987

Tabori, Paul. The Social History of Rape. London: New English Library, 1971

THE HISTORY OF RAPE

ARTICLES

Engelstein, Laura. "Gender and the Juridical Subject: Prostitution and Rape Laws in 19th-Century Russian Criminal Codes", JOURNAL OF MODERN HISTORY 60:458-495 September 1988

Lindemann, B. "'To Ravish and Carnally Know': Rape in Eighteenth-Century Massachusetts", SIGNS 10:63-82 Autumn 1984

Pistano, Stephen. "Rape in Medieval Europe", ATLANTIS 14(2):36-43 Spring 1989
_____. "Susan Brownmiller and the History of Rape", WOMEN'S STUDIES 14(3):265-276 1988

Simpson, A. "The 'Blackmail Myth' and the Prosecution of Rape and Its Attempt in 18th Century London: The Creation of a Legal Tradition", JOURNAL OF CRIMINAL LAW AND CRIMINOLOGY 77:101-150 Spring 1986

BOOKS, PAMPHLETS

Bayer, Edward. Rape within Marriage: A Moral Analysis Delayed. Lanham, MD: University Press of America, 1985

Braverman, Mara. Marital Rape. Cincinnati, OH: Pamphlet Publications, 1979 26p

Doran, Julie. Conflict and Violence in Intimate Relationships: Focus on Marital Rape. (paper presented at the annual meeting of the American Sociological Association, New York, 1980)

Economics of Marital Rape. [n.d.] [n.p.] (located in the Marital Rape Collection, University of Illinois at Urbana-Champaign)

Finkelhor, David. Common Features of Family Abuse. (paper presented at the National Conference for Family Violence Researchers, Durham, New Hampshire, July 1981)

_____. Marital Rape: The Misunderstood Crime. 1984 (address to the New York County Lawyer's Association, May 3, 1984) (available from the Family Violence Research Program, Family Research Laboratory, University of New Hampshire)

_____ and Yllo, Kersti. License to Rape: Sexual Abuse of Wives. New York: Free Press, 1987

_____ and Yllo, Kersti. The Prosecution of Marital Rape: The California Experience. 1984 (paper presented at the Second National Conference for Family Violence Researchers, Durham, New Hampshire, August, 1984) (available from the Family Violence Research Program, Family Research Laboratory, University of New Hampshire)

_____ and others, eds. The Dark Side of Families: Current Family Violence Research. Beverly Hills: Sage Publications, 1983

Fortune, Marie. Sexual Violence, the Unmentionable Sin: An Ethical and Pastoral Perspective. New York: Pilgrim Press, 1984

Frieze, Irene. Causes and Consequences of Marital Rape. (paper presented at the annual meeting of the American Psychological Association, Montreal, September 1980)

_____. Consequences of Rape in Marriage. (paper presented at the National Conference for Family Violence Researchers in Durham, New Hampshire, July 1981)

Gager, Nancy and Schurr, Cathleen. Sexual Assault: Confronting Rape in America. New York: Grosset and Dunlop, 1976 (discusses rape within marriage)

Grosfeld, Sharon. Rape within Marriage: A Sociological and Historical Analysis. (paper presented at the Society for the Psychological Study of Social Issues meetings, August 1980)

Hall, Ruth. The Rapist Who Pays the Rent: Women's Case for Changing the Law on Rape. Bristol, England: Falling Wall Press, 1984

Hutchings, Nancy, ed. The Violent Family: Victimization of Women, Children and Elders. New York: Human Sciences Press, 1988

Marital Rape Fact Sheet. [n.p.] 1985 (located in the Marital Rape Collection, University of Illinois at Urbana-Champaign)

Marital Rape: What Happens When Women Fight Back?. [n.p.] 1981 (located in the Marital Rape Collection, University of Illinois at Urbana-Champaign)

Russell, Diana. The Prevalence and Impact of Marital Rape in San Francisco. (paper presented at the American Sociological Association Meeting, New York, August 1980)

_____. Rape in Marriage. Bloomington: Indiana University Press, 1990

_____. Rape in Marriage: A Case Against Legalized Crime. (paper presented at the annual meeting of the American Society of Criminology, San Francisco, November 1980)

Shields, Nancy and Hanneke, Christine. Battered Wives' Reactions to Marital Rape. (paper presented to the National Research Conference on Family Violence, Durham, New Hampshire, 1981)

Thyfault, R. Childhood Sexual Abuse, Marital Rape, and Battered Women: Implications for Mental Health Workers. (paper presented at the annual meeting of the Colorado Mental Health Conference, Keystone, October 1980)

_____. Sexual Abuse in the Battering Relationship. (paper presented at the annual meeting of the Rocky Mountain Psychological Association, Tucson, Arizona, April 1980)

When a Husband Rapes His Wife. [n.p.] 1985 (located in the Marital Rape Collection, University of Illinois at Urbana-Champaign)

Yllo, Kersti. Types of Marital Rape: Three Case Studies. 1981 (paper presented at the National Conference for Family Violence Researchers, University of New Hampshire, July 1981) (available from the Family Violence Research Program, Family Research Laboratory, University of New Hampshire)

ARTICLES

"Abolishing the Marital Rape Exemption: The First Step in Protecting Married Women from Spousal Rape", WAYNE LAW REVIEW 35:1219-1250 Spring 1989

"Abrogation of a Common Law Sanctuary for Husband Rapists: Warren v. State", DETROIT COLLEGE OF LAW REVIEW Summer 1986, p599-612

Barshis, Victoria. "The Question of Marital Rape", WOMEN'S STUDIES INTERNATIONAL FORUM 6(4):383-393 1983

Bidwell, Lee and White, Priscilla. "The Family Context of Marital Rape", JOURNAL OF FAMILY VIOLENCE 1(3):277-287 September 1986

Bowker, Lee. "Marital Rape: A Distinct Syndrome?", SOCIAL CASEWORK 64:347-352 June 1983

Brooks, R. "Marital Consent in Rape", CRIMINAL LAW REVIEW December 1989, p877-887

Brownlee, I. "Marital Rape - Lessons from Scotland?", NEW LAW JOURNAL 139:1275-1276 September 22, 1989

Campbell, J. and Alford, P. "The Dark Consequences of Marital Rape", AMERICAN JOURNAL OF NURSING 89(7):946-949 July 1989

Chapple, Duncan. "Rape in Marriage: The South Australian Experience", in Scutt, Jocelynne, ed. Violence in the Family: A Collection of Conference Papers. Canberra: Australian Institute of Criminology, 1980, p137-144

"Constitutional Law -- The Marital Exemption in the Rape and Sodomy Statutes of the New York Penal Law and the Gender Exemption in the Rape Statute Are Unconstitutional as Violations of the Equal Protection Clause of the Fourteenth Amendment to the United States Constitution", JOURNAL OF FAMILY LAW 24:87-93 October 1985

"Criminal Law -- New York Court Abrogates Marital Rape Exemption as a Violation of Equal Protection", SUFFOLK UNIVERSITY LAW REVIEW 19:1039-1046 Winter 1985

Faulk, M. "Sexual Factors in Marital Violence", MEDICAL ASPECTS OF HUMAN SEXUALITY 11:30-43 October 1977

Finkelhor, David and Yllo, Kersti. "Forced Sex in Marriage", CRIME AND DELINQUENCY 28:459-478 1980

_____ and Yllo, Kersti. "Rape in Marriage: A Sociological View", in Finkelhor, David and others, eds. The Dark Side of Families: Current Family Violence Research. Beverly Hills, CA: Sage, 1983, p119-130

"For Better or For Worse: Marital Rape", NORTHERN KENTUCKY LAW REVIEW 15:611-643 1988

Freeman, Michael. "But If You Can't Rape Your Wife, Who Can You Rape?", FAMILY LAW QUARTERLY 15(1):1-30 Spring 1981
_____. "Doing His Best to Sustain the Sanctity of Marriage", SOCIOLOGICAL REVIEW MONOGRAPH 31:124-146 1985 (history of immunity from prosecution for marital rape in England)
Frieze, Irene. "Investigating the Causes and Consequences of Marital Rape", SIGNS 8(3):532-553 Spring 1983
Geis, Gilbert. "Rape-in-Marriage Law and Law Reform in England, the United States, and Sweden", ADELAIDE LAW REVIEW 6(2):284-303 June 1978
Gelles, Richard. "Power, Sex and Violence: The Case of Marital Rape", FAMILY COORDINATOR 26(4):339-348 October 1977
_____. "Power, Sex and Violence: The Case of Marital Rape", in Henslin, James, ed. Marriage and Family in a Changing Society. New York: Free Press, 1980, p389-402
Groth, A. and Gary, Thomas. "Marital Rape", MEDICAL ASPECTS OF HUMAN SEXUALITY 15(3):122-132 March 1981
Hanneke, Christine and Shields, Nancy. "Marital Rape: Implications for the Helping Professions", SOCIAL CASEWORK 66(8):451-458 October 1985
_____ and others. "Assessing the Prevalence of Marital Rape", JOURNAL OF INTERPERSONAL VIOLENCE 1(3):350-362 September 1986
Harman, J. "Consent, Harm, and Marital Rape", JOURNAL OF FAMILY LAW 22(3):423-443 April 1984
"The Injustice of the Marital Rape Exemption: A Survey of Common Law Countries", AMERICAN UNIVERSITY JOURNAL OF INTERNATIONAL LAW AND POLICY 4:555-589 Summer 1989
Jeffords, Charles. "The Impact of Sex-Role and Religious Attitudes upon Forced Marital Intercourse Norms", SEX ROLES 11(5/6):543-552 September 1984
_____. "Prosecutorial Discretion in Cases of Marital Rape", VICTIMOLOGY 9(3/4):415-425 1984
_____ and Dull, R. "Demographic Variations in Attitudes Towards Marital Rape Immunity", JOURNAL OF MARRIAGE AND THE FAMILY 44(3):755-762 August 1982
"The Marital Rape Exemption: Time for Legal Reform", TULSA LAW JOURNAL 21:353-384 1985
Mettger, Zak. "A Case of Rape: Forced Sex in Marriage", RESPONSE TO FAMILY VIOLENCE AND SEXUAL ASSAULT 5:1+ March/April 1982
Noonan, Jean and Conner, Diane. "All in the Family: Rape, Battering and Incest", AEGIS Summer 1982, p31-38
"Problems of Convicting a Husband for the Rape of His Wife", NOVA LAW JOURNAL 9:351-380 Winter 1985
Scheyett, Anna. "Marriage Is the Best Defense: Policy on Marital Rape", AFFILIA 3(4):8-23 Winter 1988

"Sexism and the Common Law: Spousal Rape in Virginia", GEORGE MASON UNIVERSITY LAW REVIEW 8:369-387 Spring 1986

"Sexual Assault: The Case for Removing the Spousal Exemption from Texas Law", BAYLOR LAW REVIEW 38:1041-1062 Fall 1986

Shields, Nancy and Hanneke, Christine. "Battered Wives' Reactions to Martial Rape", in Finkelhor, David and others, eds. The Dark Side of Families: Current Family Violence Research. Beverly Hills, CA: Sage 1983, p131-148

Sigler, Robert and Haygood, Donna. "The Criminalization of Forced Marital Intercourse", MARRIAGE AND FAMILY REVIEW 12(1/2):71-85 1987

Slovenko, Ralph. "Rape of a Wife by Her Husband", MEDICAL ASPECTS OF HUMAN SEXUALITY July 1974, p65+

"Spousal Sexual Assault: Pennsylvania's Place on the Sliding Scale of Protection from Marital Rape", DICKINSON LAW REVIEW 90:777-801 Summer 1986

"To Have and to Hold: The Marital Rape Exemption and the Fourteenth Amendment", HARVARD LAW REVIEW 99(6):1255-1273 April 1986

Waterman, Sallee. "For Better or for Worse: Marital Rape", NORTHERN KENTUCKY LAW REVIEW 15(3):611-643 1988

Weingourt, Rita. "Wife Rape: Barriers to Indentification and Treatment", AMERICAN JOURNAL OF PSYCHOTHERAPY 39(2):187-192 April 1985

Yegidis, Bonnie. "Wife Abuse and Marital Rape among Women Who Seek Help", AFFILIA 3(1):62-68 Spring 1988

Yllo, Kersti and Finkelhor, David. "Marital Rape", in Burgess, A., ed. Rape and Sexual Assault: A Research Handbook. New York: Garland, 1985, p146-158

DATE AND ACQUAINTANCE RAPE

BOOKS, PAMPHLETS

Adams, Caren and Fay, Jennifer. "Nobody Told Me It Was Rape": A Parent's Guide for Talking with Teenagers. Santa Cruz, CA: Network Publications, 1984 30p

Bateman, Py and Stringer, Gayle. Where Do I Start?: A Parents' Guide for Talking to Teens about Acquaintance Rape. 1984 60p (available from ERIC, No.ED296244)

Ehrhart, Julie and Sandler, Bernice. Campus Gang Rape: Party Games? Washington, DC: Association of American Colleges, 1985 22p

Floerchinger, Debra. Dating Can Be Dangerous: A Program Assessing Student Attitudes on Campus. 1988 57p (available from ERIC, No.ED305534)

Hughes, Jean and Sandler, Bernice. "Friends" Raping Friends: Could It Happen to You? Washington, DC: Association of American Colleges, 1987 9p

McShane, Claudette. Warning! Dating May Be Hazardous to Your Health. Racine, WI: Mother Courage Press, 1988

Pirog-Good, Maureen and Stets, Jan, eds. Violence in Dating Relationships: Emerging Social Issues. New York: Praeger, 1989

Rue, Nancy. Coping with Dating Violence. New York: Rosen Publishing Group, 1989

Sanday, Peggy. Fraternity Gang Rape: Sex, Brotherhood and Privilege on Campus. New York: New York University Press, 1990

Warshaw, Robin. I Never Called it Rape: The Ms. Report on Recognizing, Fighting, and Surviving Date and Acquaintance Rape. New York: Harper and Row, 1988

ARTICLES

Aizenman, Marta and Kelley, Georgette. "The Incidence of Violence and Acquaintance Rape in Dating Relationships among College Men and Women", JOURNAL OF COLLEGE STUDENT DEVELOPMENT 29(4):305-311 July 1988

Bridges, J. and McGrail, C. "Attributions of Responsibility for Date and Stranger Rape", SEX ROLES 2(3/4):273-286 August 1989

Burke, P. and others. "Gender Identity, Self-Esteem, and Physical and Sexual Abuse in Dating Relationships", SOCIAL PSYCHOLOGY QUARTERLY 51:272-285 September 1988

Campbell, Jacquelyn. "Women's Responses to Sexual Abuse in Intimate Relationships", HEALTH CARE FOR WOMEN INTERNATIONAL 10(4):335+ 1989

Coller, Sarah and Resick, Patricia. "Women's Attributions of Responsibility for Date Rape: The Influence of Empathy and Sex-Role Stereotyping", VIOLENCE AND VICTIMS 2(2):115-125 Spring 1987

Dull, R. and Giacopassi, David. "Demographic Correlates of Sexual and Dating Attitudes: A Study of Date Rape", CRIMINAL JUSTICE AND BEHAVIOR 14(2):175-193 June 1987

Ehrhart, Julie and Sandler, Bernice. "Party Rape", RESPONSE TO THE VICTIMIZATION OF WOMEN AND CHILDREN 9(1):2-5 1986

Fischer, Gloria. "College Student Attitudes Toward Forcible Date Rape: Changes after Taking a Human Sexuality Course", 12(1):42-46 Spring/Summer 1986

_____. "College Student Attitudes Toward Forcible Date Rape: I. Cognitive Predictors", ARCHIVES OF SEXUAL BEHAVIOR 15(6):457-466 December 1986

_____. "Hispanic and Majority Student Attitudes Toward Forcible Date Rape as a Function of Differences in Attitudes Toward Women", SEX ROLES 17(1/2):93-101 July 1987

Gray, M. and others. "The Effectiveness of Personalizing Acquaintance Rape Prevention: Programs on Perception of Vulnerability and on Reducing Risk-Taking Behavior", JOURNAL OF COLLEGE STUDENT DEVELOPMENT 31(3):217-220 May 1990

Jenkins, Megan and Dambrot, Faye. "The Attribution of Date Rape: Observer's Attitudes and Sexual Experiences and the Dating Situation", JOURNAL OF APPLIED SOCIAL PSYCHOLOGY 17(10):875-895 October 1987

Johnson, James and Jackson, Lee. "Assessing the Effects of Factors that Might Underlie the Differential Perception of Acquaintance and Stranger Rape", SEX ROLES 19(1/2):37-45 July 1988

_____ **and Russ, I.** "Effects of Salience of Consciousness-Raising Information on Perceptions of Acquaintance Versus Stranger Rape", JOURNAL OF APPLIED SOCIAL PSYCHOLOGY 19:1182-1197 October 1989

Kanin, Eugene. "Date Rape: Unofficial Criminals and Victims", VICTIMOLOGY 9(1):95-108 1984

_____ . "Date Rapists: Differential Sexual Socialization and Relative Deprivation", ARCHIVES OF SEXUAL BEHAVIOR 14(3):218-232 June 1985

_____ . "Rape as a Function of Relative Sexual Frustration", PSYCHOLOGICAL REPORTS 52(1):133-134 February 1983

Koss, Mary and others. "Stranger and Acquaintance Rape: Are There Differences in the Victim's Experience", PSYCHOLOGY OF WOMEN QUARTERLY 12(1):1-24 March 1988

Levine, Edward and Kanin, Eugene. "Sexual Violence among Date and Acquaintances: Trends and Their Implications for Marriage and Family", JOURNAL OF FAMILY VIOLENCE 2(1):55-65 March 1987

Levine-MacCombie, Joyce and Koss, Mary. "Acquaintance Rape: Effective Avoidance Strategies", PSYCHOLOGY OF WOMEN QUARTERLY 10(4):311-320 December 1986

Martin, Patricia and Hummer, Robert. "Fraternities and Rape on Campus", GENDER AND SOCIETY 3(4):457+ December 1989

McDermott, Robert and others. "Nonconsensual Sex among University Students: A Multivariate Analysis", HEALTH EDUCATION RESEARCH 3(3):233-241 September 1988

Meer, J. "Date Rape: Familiar Strangers", PSYCHOLOGY TODAY 21:10 July 1987

Miller, Beverly. "Date Rape: Time for a New Look at Prevention", JOURNAL OF COLLEGE STUDENT DEVELOPMENT 29(6):553-555 November 1988

_____ **and Marshall, Jon.** "Coercive Sex on the University Campus", JOURNAL OF COLLEGE STUDENT PERSONNEL 28(1):38-47 January 1987

Muehlenhard, Charlene. "Misinterpreted Dating Behaviors and the Risk of Date Rape", JOURNAL OF SOCIAL AND CLINICAL PSYCHOLOGY 6(1):20-37 1988

_____ **and Linton, Melaney.** "Date Rape and Sexual Aggression in Dating Situations: Incidence and Risk Factors", JOURNAL OF COUNSELING PSYCHOLOGY 34(2):186-196 April 1987

_____ **and others.** "Is Date Rape Justifiable? The Effects of Dating Activity, Who Initiated, Who Paid, and Men's Attitudes Toward Women", PSYCHOLOGY OF WOMEN QUARTERLY 9(3):297-309 September 1985

Neff, Laurie. "Acquaintance Rape on Campus: The Problem, the Victims, and Prevention", NASPA JOURNAL 25(3):146-152 Winter 1988

Parrot, A. "Acquaintance Rape among Adolescents: Identifying Risk Groups and Intervention Strategies", JOURNAL OF SOCIAL WORK AND HUMAN SEXUALITY 8(1):47-61 1989

_____. "Why Nice Men Force Rape on Their Friends: The Problem of Acquaintance Rape", HUMAN ECOLOGY FORUM 14(4):17-18 1984

Pineau, L. "Date Rape -- A Feminist Analysis", LAW AND PHILOSOPHY 8(2):217-243 August 1989

Renner, K. and Wackett, Carol. "Sexual Assault: Social and Stranger Rape", CANADIAN JOURNAL OF COMMUNITY MENTAL HEALTH 6(1):49-56 Spring 1987

Shotland, R. "A Preliminary Model of Some Causes of Date Rape", ACADEMIC PSYCHOLOGY BULLETIN 7(2):187-200 Summer 1985

_____ **and Goodstein, Lynne.** "Just Because She Doesn't Want to Doesn't Mean It's Rape: An Experimentally Based Causal Model of the Perception of Rape in a Dating Situation", SOCIAL PSYCHOLOGY QUARTERLY 46(3):220-232 September 1983

Stets, J. and Pirog-Good, M. "Sexual Aggression and Control in Dating Relationships", JOURNAL OF APPLIED SOCIAL PSYCHOLOGY 19:1392-1412 November 1989

Sweet, Ellen. "Date Rape: The Story of an Epidemic and Those Who Deny It", MS 14:56+ October 1985

Tetreault, Patricia and Barnett, Mark. "Reactions to Stranger and Acquaintance Rape", PSYCHOLOGY OF WOMEN QUARTERLY 11(3):353-358 September 1987

Yegidis, Bonnie. "Date Rape and Other Forced Sexual Encounters among College Students", JOURNAL OF SEX EDUCATION AND THERAPY 12(2):51-54 Fall/Winter 1986

MALE RAPE

BOOKS

Brownmiller, Susan. Against Our Will. New York: Simon and Schuster, 1975

Porter, E. Treating the Young Male Victim of Sexual Assault: Issues and Intervention Strategies. Syracuse, NH: Safer Society Press, 1986

Scacco, Anthony. Male Rape. New York: AMS Press, 1982

Weiss, Carl and Friar, David. Terror in the Prisons: Homosexual Rape and Why Society Codons It. New York: Bobbs Merrill, 1974

Wooden, Wayne and Parker, Jay. Men Behind Bars: Sexual Exploitation in Prison. New York: Plenum Press, 1982

MALE RAPE

ARTICLES

Cahill, Tom. "Cruel and Unusual Punishment: Rape in Prison", VICTIMOLOGY 9(1):8-10 1984

_____. "Prison Rape: Society's Tool for Political Control of Inmates", (SAN FRANCISCO) BAY AREA REPORTER August 8, 1985

_____. "Prison Rape: Torture in the American Gulag", in Abbott, Franklin, ed. Men and Intimacy. Freedom, CA: The Crossing Press, 1990

_____. "Rape Behind Bars", THE PROGRESSIVE 49(11):32-34 November 1985

_____. "Rape Behind Bars: A Victim's Analysis", THE CALIFORNIA PRISONER Volume 16, September 1987

_____. "Torture -- In the American Gulag: The Rape of Men Behind Bars", M/R 3:3+ January/February 1989

Calderwood, Deryck. "The Male Rape Victim", MEDICAL ASPECTS OF HUMAN SEXUALITY 21(5):53-55 May 1987

Cotton, Donald and Groth, A. "Inmate Rape: Prevention and Intervention", JOURNAL OF PRISON AND JAIL HEALTH 2(1):47-57 Spring/Summer 1982

Forman, Bruce. "Reported Male Rape", VICTIMOLOGY 7(1-4):235-236 1982

French, Lawrence. "The Perversion of Incarceration: A Social-Psychological Perspective", CORRECTIVE AND SOCIAL PSYCHIATRY AND JOURNAL OF BEHAVIOR TECHNOLOGY: METHODS AND THERAPY 24(1):16-19 1978 (focuses upon the issue of correctional sexploitation)

Goyer, Peter and Eddleman, Henry. "Same-Sex Rape of Nonincarcerated Men", AMERICAN JOURNAL OF PSYCHIATRY 141(4):576-579 April 1984

Groth, A. and Burgess, Ann. "Male Rape: Offenders and Victims", AMERICAN JOURNAL OF PSYCHIATRY 137(7):806-810 July 1980

Hinckle, Warren. "The Shame of Our Prisons: Unprevented, Unpunished Rape", SAN FRANCISCO EXAMINER January 13, 1986

Kaszniak, Alfred and others. "Amnesia as a Consequence of Male Rape: A Case Report", JOURNAL OF ABNORMAL PSYCHOLOGY 97(1):100-104 February 1988

Kaufman, Arthur and others. "Male Rape Victims: Noninstitutionalized Assault", AMERICAN JOURNAL OF PSYCHIATRY 137(2):221-223 February 1980

Masters, William. "Sexual Dysfunction as an Aftermath of Sexual Assault of Men by Women", JOURNAL OF SEX AND MARITAL THERAPY 12(1):35-45 Spring 1986

Mezey, Gillian and King, Michael. "The Effects of Sexual Assault on Men: A Survey of 22 Victims", PSYCHOLOGICAL MEDICINE 19(1):205-209 February 1989

Money, John and Bohmer, Carol. "Prison Sexology: Two Personal Accounts of Masturbation, Homosexuality, and Rape", JOURNAL OF SEX RESEARCH 16(3):258-266 August 1980

Moss, C. and others. "Sexual Assault in a Prison", PSYCHOLOGICAL REPORTS 44(3):823-828 June 1979

Myers, M. "Men Sexually Assaulted as Adults and Sexually Abused as Boys", ARCHIVES OF SEXUAL BEHAVIOR 18:203-215 June 1989

Nacci, Peter and Kane, Thomas. "The Incidence of Sex and Sexual Aggression in Federal Prisons", FEDERAL PROBATION 47(4):31-36 December 1983

_____ and Kane, Thomas. "Inmate Sexual Aggression: Some Evolving Propositions, Empirical Findings, and Mitigating Counter-Forces", JOURNAL OF OFFENDER COUNSELING, SERVICES AND REHABILITATION 9(1/2):1-20 Fall/Winter 1984

Price, John. "Homosexuality in a Victorian Male Prison", MENTAL HEALTH IN AUSTRALIA 1(12):3-12 July 1984

Rothenberg, David. "As If Imprisonment Itself Is Not Horrendous Enough", NEW YORK TIMES January 29, 1977

Siemaszko, Corky. "Prison Rape Common, but Ignored", KIPLINGER PROGRAM REPORT Summer 1989

Smith, Ronald and others. "Social Cognitions about Adult Male Victims of Female Sexual Assault", JOURNAL OF SEX RESEARCH 24:101-112 1988

Smith, Russell. "The 'Corrections' System: A Rape Victim's Point of View", PRISON LAW MONITOR November/December 1979

Starr, Kevin. "Rape in Prison", SAN FRANCISCO EXAMINER May 28, 1982

Struckman-Johnson, Cindy. "Forced Sex on Dates: It Happens to Men, Too", JOURNAL OF SEX RESEARCH 24:234-241 1988

Vander Mey, B. "The Sexual Victimization of Male Children: A Review of Previous Research", CHILD ABUSE AND NEGLECT: THE INTERNATIONAL JOURNAL 12(1):61-72 1988

Wiggs, J. "Prison Rape and Suicide", JOURNAL OF THE AMERICAN MEDICAL ASSOCIATION 262(24):3403 December 22, 1989
Salive, M. and others. "Prison Rape and Suicide -- Reply", JOURNAL OF THE AMERICAN MEDICAL ASSOCIATION 262(24):3403 December 22, 1989

PSYCHOLOGICAL IMPACT OF RAPE ON THE VICTIM

BOOKS AND PAMPHLETS

Adams, Caren and Fay, Jennifer. Free of the Shadows: Recovering from Sexual Violence. Oakland, CA: New Harbinger Publications, 1989

Bode, Janet. Fighting Back: How to Cope with the Medical, Emotional, and Legal Consequences of Rape. New York: Macmillan, 1978

Burgess, Ann and Holmstrom, Lynda. Rape, Crisis and Recovery. Bowie, MD: R.J. Brady, 1979

Carmen, Elaine. The Rape Victim. New York: Basic Books, 1976

Ellis, Megan. Surviving Procedures after a Sexual Assault. Vancouver: Press Gang Publishers, 1988

Grossman, Rochel and Sutherland, Joan, eds. Surviving Sexual Assault. New York: Congdon and Weed, 1983 86p

Katz, Judy. No Fairy Godmothers, No Magic Wands: The Healing Process after Rape. Saratoga, CA: R&E Publishers, 1984

Kelly, Liz. Surviving Sexual Violence. Minneapolis: University of Minnesota Press, 1988

Ledray, Linda. Recovering from Rape. New York: H. Holt, 1986

Nass, Deanna, ed. The Rape Victim. Dubuque, Iowa: Kendall/Hunt Publishing, 1977

Portwood, Pamela and others, eds. Rebirth of Power: Overcoming the Effects of Sexual Abuse through the Experiences of Others. Racine, WI: Mother Courage Press, 1987

Roth, Susan and Others. Victimization History and Victim-Assailant Relationship as Factors in Recovery from Sexual Assault. 1988 21p (Paper presented at the Southeastern Psychological Association, 1988) (available from ERIC, No.ED296269)

Rothbaum, Barbara and others. Responses Following Sexual and Non-Sexual Assault. 1988 10p (Paper presented at the Association for the Advancement of Behavior Therapy) (available from ERIC, No.ED310346)

Walters, Candance. Invisible Wounds: What Every Woman Should Know about Sexual Assault. Portland, OR: Multnomah, 1988

PSYCHOLOGICAL IMPACT OF RAPE ON THE VICTIM

ARTICLES

Becker, Judith and others. "Level of Postassault Sexual Functioning in Rape and Incest Victims", ARCHIVES OF SEXUAL BEHAVIOR 15(1):37-49 February 1986

Burge, Sandra. "Post-Traumatic Stress Disorder in Victims of Rape", JOURNAL OF TRAUMATIC STRESS 1(2):193-210 April 1988

Burt, Martha and Katz, Bonnie. "Dimensions of Recovery from Rape: Focus on Growth Outcomes", JOURNAL OF INTERPERSONAL VIOLENCE 2(1):57-81 1987

Cohen, Lawrence and Roth, Susan. "The Psychological Aftermath of Rape: Long-Term Effects and Individual Differences in Recovering", JOURNAL OF SOCIAL AND CLINICAL PSYCHOLOGY 5(4):525-534 1987

Coons, P. and Milstein, V. "Rape and Post-Traumatic Stress in Multiple Personality", PSYCHOLOGICAL REPORTS 55:839-845 December 1984

DiVasto, Peter. "Measuring the Aftermath of Rape", JOURNAL OF PSYCHOSOCIAL NURSING AND MENTAL HEALTH SERVICES 23(2):33-35 February 1985

Emm, Deborah and McKenry, Patrick. "Coping with Victimization: The Impact of Rape on Female Survivors, Male Significant Others, and Parents", CONTEMPORARY FAMILY THERAPY: AN INTERNATIONAL JOURNAL 10(4):272-279 Winter 1988

Forman, Bruce. "Assessing the Impact of Rape and Its Significance in Psychotherapy", PSYCHOTHERAPY: THEORY, RESEARCH AND PRACTICE 20(4):515-519 Winter 1983

Frank, Ellen and Anderson, Barbara. "Psychiatric Disorders in Rape Victims: Past History and Current Symptomatology", COMPREHENSIVE PSYCHIATRY 28(1):77-82 January/February 1987

Gilbert, Barbara and Cunningham, Jean. "Women's Postrape Sexual Functioning: Review and Implications for Counseling", JOURNAL OF COUNSELING AND DEVELOPMENT 65(2):71-73 October 1986

Gilmartin-Zena, Pat. "Rape Impact: Immediately and Two Months Later", DEVIANT BEHAVIOR 6(4):347-361 1985

Girelli, Steven and others. "Subjective Distress and Violence During Rape: Their Effects on Long-Term Fear", VIOLENCE AND VICTIMS 1(1):35-46 Spring 1986

Gise, Leslie and Paddison, Patricia. "Rape, Sexual Abuse, and Its Victims", PSYCHIATRIC CLINICS OF NORTH AMERICA 11(4):629-648 December 1988

Greenspan, Gail and Samuel, Steven. "Self-Cutting after Rape", AMERICAN JOURNAL OF PSYCHIATRY 146(6):789-790 June 1989

Jacobson, A. "Physical and Sexual Assault Histories among Psychiatric Outpatients", AMERICAN JOURNAL OF PSYCHIATRY 146:755-758 June 1989

Jenny, C. and others. "Sexually Transmitted Diseases in Victims of Rape", NEW ENGLAND JOURNAL OF MEDICINE 322(11):713-716 March 15, 1990

Koss, Mary. "The Hidden Rape Victim: Personality, Attitudinal and Situational Characteristics", PSYCHOLOGY OF WOMEN QUARTERLY 9:193-212 June 1985

_____ and Burkhart, Barry. "A Conceptual Analysis of Rape Victimization: Long-Term Effects and Implications for Treatment", PSYCHOLOGY OF WOMEN QUARTERLY 13(1):27-40 March 1989

Lenox, Michelle and Gannon, Linda. "Psychological Consequences of Rape and Variables Influencing Recovery: A Review", WOMEN AND THERAPY 2:37-49 September 1983

Marhoefer-Dvorak, Susan and others. "Single- Versus Multiple-Incident Rape Victims: A Comparison of Psychological Reactions to Rape", JOURNAL OF INTERPERSONAL VIOLENCE 3(2):145-160 June 1988

Marton, F. "Defenses: Invincible and Vincible [Rape Trauma Syndrome]", CLINICAL SOCIAL WORK JOURNAL 16:143-155 Summer 1988

Meyer, C. and Taylor, Shelley. "Adjustment to Rape", JOURNAL OF PERSONALITY AND SOCIAL PSYCHOLOGY 50(6):1226-1234 June 1986

Mezey, Gillian and Taylor, Pamela. "Psychological Reactions of Women Who Have Been Raped: A Descriptive and Comparative Study", BRITISH JOURNAL OF PSYCHIATRY 152:330-339 March 1988

Murphy, Shane and others. "Rape Victims' Self-Esteem: A Longitudinal Analysis", JOURNAL OF INTERPERSONAL VIOLENCE 3(4):355-370 December 1988

Myers, M. and others. "Coping Ability of Women Who Become Victims of Rape", JOURNAL OF CONSULTING CLINICAL PSYCHOLOGY 52:73-78 February 1984
Discussion. JOURNAL OF CONSULTING CLINICAL PSYCHOLOGY 53:429-431 June 1985

Popiel, Debra and Susskind, Edwin. "The Impact of Rape: Social Support as a Moderator of Stress", AMERICAN JOURNAL OF COMMUNITY PSYCHOLOGY 13(6):645-676 December 1985

Root, M. "Treatment Failures: The Role of Sexual Victimization in Women's Addictive Behavior", AMERICAN JOURNAL OF ORTHOPSYCHIATRY 59:542-549 October 1989

Rose, Deborah. "'Worse than Death': Psychodynamics of Rape Victims and the Need for Psychotherapy", AMERICAN JOURNAL OF PSYCHIATRY 143(7):817-824 July 1986
Discussion. AMERICAN JOURNAL OF PSYCHIATRY 144:541 April 1987

Rosenberg, Marcia. "Rape Crisis Syndrome", MEDICAL ASPECTS OF HUMAN SEXUALITY 20(3):65-71 March 1986

Roth, Susan and Lebowitz, Leslie. "The Experience of Sexual Trauma", JOURNAL OF TRAUMATIC STRESS 1(1):79-107 January 1988

Rynd, Nancy. "Incidence of Psychometric Symptoms in Rape Victims", JOURNAL OF SEX RESEARCH 24:155-161 1988

Sales, E. and others. "Victim Readjustment Following Assault", JOURNAL OF SOCIAL ISSUES 40:117-136 Spring 1984

Santiago, Jose and others. "Long-Term Psychological Effects of Rape in 35 Rape Victims", AMERICAN JOURNAL OF PSYCHIATRY 142(11):1338-1340 November 1985

Steketee, Gail and Foa, Edna. "Rape Victims: Post-Traumatic Stress Responses and Their Treatment: A Review of the Literature", JOURNAL OF ANXIETY DISORDERS 1(1):69-86 1987

Stewart, Barbara and others. "The Aftermath of Rape: Profiles of Immediate and Delayed Treatment Seekers", JOURNAL OF NERVOUS AND MENTAL DISEASE 175(2):90-94 February 1987

Thorton, B. and others. "Reaction to Self-Attributed Victim Responsibility: A Comparative Analysis of Rape Crisis Counselors and Lay Observers", JOURNAL OF APPLIED SOCIAL PSYCHOLOGY 18:409-422 April 1988

Waigandt, C. and Miller, Deborah. "Maladaptive Responses During the Reorganization Phase of Rape Trauma Syndrome", RESPONSE TO THE VICTIMIZATION OF WOMEN AND CHILDREN 9(2):20-21 1986

Ward, Colleen. "Stress, Coping and Adjustment in Victims of Sexual Assault: The Role of Psychological Defense Mechanisms", COUNSELING PSYCHOLOGY QUARTERLY 1(2/3):165-178 1988

Weidner, G. and Griffitt, W. "Rape: A Sexual Stigma?", JOURNAL OF PERSONALITY 51:152-166 June 1983

Wright, Rogers. "Of Slithy Toves, Rape-Trauma Syndrome, Burn-Out, etc.", PSYCHOTHERAPY IN PRIVATE PRACTICE 3(1):99-108 Spring 1985

BOOKS, PAMPHLETS

Calhoun, Daren and Atkeson, Beverly. Treatment of Rape Victims. New York: Pergamon Press, 1989

Foley, Theresa and Davies, Marilyn. Rape: Nursing Care for Victims. St. Louis: Mosby, 1983

Getzel, George. Violence: Prevention and Treatment in Groups. Binghamton, NY: Haworth Press, 1989

Green, William. Rape: The Evidential Examination and Management of the Adult Female Victim. Lexington, MA: Lexington Books, 1988

Halpern, Susan and others, eds. Rape: Helping the Victim: A Treatment Manual. Oradell, NJ: Medical Economics, 1978

Holmstrom, Lynda and Burgess, Ann. The Victim of Rape: Institutional Reactions. New Brunswick, NJ: Transaction Books, 1983

How to Start a Rape Crisis Center. Washington, DC: Rape Crisis Center, 1974 43p

Kluft, Richard, ed. Treatment of Victims of Sexual Abuse. Philadelphia, PA: Saunders, 1989

Koss, Mary and Harvey, Mary. The Rape Victim: Clinical and Community Approaches to Treatment. Lexington, MA: S. Greene Press, 1987

Koss, Mary and others. Clinical Treatment of Nonrecent Rape: How Much Do We Know? 1985 24p (Research sponsored by United States, Department of Health and Human Services, Nation Center for the Control and Prevention of Rape) (available from ERIC, No.ED267320)

Laidlaw, Toni Ann and Malmo, Cheryl. Healing Voices: Feminist Approaches to Therapy with Women. San Francisco: Jossey-Bass, 1990

Lynch, Sherry. Counseling Date Rape Survivors: Implications for College Student Personnel Professionals. 1985 17p (Paper presented at the American College Personnel Association, 1985) (available for ERIC, No.ED267319)

McCombie, Sharon, ed. The Rape Crisis Intervention Handbook: A Guide for Victim Care. New York: Plenum Press, 1980

Quina, Kathryn and Carlson, Nancy. Rape, Incest, and Sexual Harrassment: A Guide for Helping Survivors. New York: Praeger, 1989

Rodabaugh, Barbara and Austin, Melanie. Sexual Assault: A Guide for Community Action. New York: Garland STPM Press, 1981

Smith, Steven and Freinkel, Susan. Adjusting the Balance: Federal Policy and Victim Services. Westport, CT: Greenwood, 1988

Stevens, D. "Violence Against Women: Rape Victims" in Gottlieb, Naomi, ed. Alternative Social Services for Women. New York: Columbia University Press, 1980

Stuart, Irving and Greer, Joanne, eds. Victims of Sexual Aggression: Treatment of Children, Women, and Men. New York: Van Nostrand Reinhold, 1984

Warner, Carmen, ed. Rape and Sexual Assault. Germantown, MD: Aspen Systems Corporation, 1980

_____ and Braen, G., eds. Management of the Physically and Emotionally Abused: Emergency Assessment, Intervention, and Counseling. Norwalk, CT: Appleton Century Crofts, 1982

TREATMENT AND SERVICES FOR RAPE VICTIMS

ARTICLES

Bateman, Anthony. "Helping the Partners of Rape Victims", SEXUAL AND MARITAL THERAPY 4(1):5-7 1989

Burt, M. and Gornick, J. "Ten Years After: Rape Crisis Centers", OFF OUR BACKS 14(8):17-22 1984

Colao, Flora and Hunt, Miriam. "Therapists Coping with Sexual Assault", WOMEN AND THERAPY 2:205-214 Summer/Fall 1983

Collins, Barbara and Whalen, Mary. "The Rape Crisis Movement: Radical or Reformist?", SOCIAL WORK 34(1):61-63 January 1989

Dennis, Louise. "Adolescent Rape: The Role of Nursing", ISSUES IN COMPREHENSIVE PEDIATRIC NURSING 11(1):59-70 1988

Ebert, Bruce. "Hypnosis and Rape Victims", AMERICAN JOURNAL OF CLINICAL HYPNOSIS 31(1):50-56 July 1988

Feinauer, Leslie and Hippolite, Debbie. "Once a Princess, Always a Princess: A Strategy for Therapy with Families of Rape Victims", CONTEMPORARY FAMILY THERAPY: AN INTERNATIONAL JOURNAL 9(4):252-262 Winter 1987

Feldman-Summers, S. and Norris, J. "Differences Between Rape Victims Who Report and Those Who Do Not Report to a Public Agency", JOURNAL OF APPLIED SOCIAL PSYCHOLOGY 14:562-573 November/December 1984

Frank, Ellen and others. "Efficacy of Cognitive Behavior Therapy and Systematic Desensitization in the Treatment of Rape", BEHAVIOR THERAPY 19(3):403-420 Summer 1988

Gilbert, Barbara and Cunningham, Jean. "Women's Postrape Sexual Functioning: Review and Implications for Counseling", JOURNAL OF COUNSELING AND DEVELOPMENT 65(2):71-73 October 1986

Golding, Jacqueline and others. "Sexual Assault History and Use of Health and Mental Health Services", AMERICAN JOURNAL OF COMMUNITY PSYCHOLOGY 16:625-644 October 1988

_____ **and others.** "Social Support Sources Following Sexual Assault", JOURNAL OF COMMUNITY PSYCHOLOGY 17(1):92-107 January 1989

Gornick, Janet and others. "Structure and Activities of Rape Crisis Centers in the Early 1980's", CRIME AND DELINQUENCY 31(2):247-268 April 1985

Gurley, Gail. "Counseling the Rape Victim's Loved Ones", RESPONSE TO THE VICTIMIZATION OF WOMEN AND CHILDREN 9(4):8-9 1986

Jacobs, Janet. "The Effects of Ritual Healing on Female Victims of Abuse: A Study of Empowerment and Transformation", SOCIOLOGICAL ANALYSIS 50(3):265-279 Fall 1989

Kilpatrick, Dean and Calhoun, Karen. "Early Behavior Treatment for Rape Trauma: Efficacy or Artifact?", BEHAVIOR THERAPY 19(3):421-427 Summer 1988

Koss, Mary and Burkhart, Barry. "A Conceptual Analysis of Rape Victimization: Long-Term Effects and Implications for Treatment", PSYCHOLOGY OF WOMEN QUARTERLY 13(1):27-40 March 1989

Koziey, Paul and McLeod, Gordon. "Visual Kinesthetic Dissociation in Treatment of Victims of Rape", PROFESSIONAL PSYCHOLOGY RESEARCH AND PRACTICE 18(3):276-282 June 1987

Martin, Particia and DiNitto, Diana. "The Rape Exam: Beyond the Hospital Emergency Room", WOMEN AND HEALTH 12(2):5-28 1987

_____ **and others.** "Controversies Surrounding the Rape Kit Exam in the 1980's: Issues and Alternatives", CRIME AND DELINQUENCY 31(2):223-246 April 1985

Mills, J. "The Initial Interview of Sexual Assault Victims: A Humanistic Approach to Investigation", POLICE CHIEF 56:119-122 April 1989

Orzek, Ann. "The Lesbian Victim of Sexual Assault: Special Considerations for the Mental Health Professional", WOMEN AND THERAPY 8(1/2):107-117 1988

Perl, Mark and others. "The Female Rape Survivor: Time-Limited Group Therapy with Female-Male Co-Therapists", JOURNAL OF PSYCHOSOMATIC, OBSTETRICS AND GYNECOLOGY 4(3):197-205 September 1985

Renshaw, Domeena. "Treatment of Sexual Exploitation: Rape and Incest", PSYCHIATRIC CLINICS OF NORTH AMERICA 12(2):257-277 June 1989

Resick, Patricia and others. "A Comparative Outcome Study of Behavioral Group Therapy for Sexual Assault Victims", BEHAVIOR THERAPY 19(3):385-401 Summer 1988

Sharma, Anu and Cheatham, Harold. "A Women's Center Support Group for Sexual Assault Victims", JOURNAL OF COUNSELING AND DEVELOPMENT 64(8):525-527 April 1986

Smith, Catherine and Marcus, Philip.   "Structural Persistence in Proactive Organizations: The Case of Sexual Assault Treatment Agencies", JOURNAL OF SOCIAL SERVICE RESEARCH 7(4):21-36 Summer 1984

Steketee, Gail and Foa, Edna. "Rape Victims: Post-Traumatic Stress Responses and Their Treatment: A Review of the Literature", JOURNAL OF ANXIETY DISORDERS 1(1):69-86 1987

Waterman, C. and others. "Sexual Coercion in Gay Male and Lesbian Relationships: Predictors and Implications for Support Services", JOURNAL OF SEX RESEARCH 26:118-124 February 1989

Wirtz, P. and Harrell, A. "Effects of Postassault Exposure to Attack-Similar Stimuli on Long-Term Recovery of Victims", JOURNAL OF CONSULTING AND CLINICAL PSYCHOLOGY 55:10-16 February 1987

Xenarios, Susan. "Sounds of Practice I: Group Work with Rape Survivors", SOCIAL WORK WITH GROUPS 11(3):95-100 1988

Yassen, J. and Glass, L. "Sexual Assault Survivors Groups: A Feminist Practice Perspective", SOCIAL WORK 29:252-257 May/June 1984

BOOKS, PAMPHLETS

Bourque, Linda. Defining Rape. Durham, NC: Duke University Press, 1989

Burt, Martha. Cultural Myths and Supports for Rape. Washington, DC: Urban Institute, 1980

Carducci, Bernardo. Affective and Attributional Reactions to Sexual Harassment as Determined by Outcome. 1987 10p (Paper presented at the Western Psychological Association, 1987) (available from ERIC, No.ED282118)

Chen, Jeaw-Mei and Lin, Phylis. American College Students' Attitudes toward Rape Victims and Beliefs in a Just World. 1988 31p (available from ERIC, No.ED305290)

Dowdeswell, Jane. Women on Rape. New York: Thorsons Publishing Group, 1986

Larson, Knud and Long, Ed. Attitudes toward Rape. 1987 18p (Paper presented at the Western Psychological Association, 1987) (available from ERIC, No.ED278884)

Lubomski, Lisa and others. Defensive Attributions of Rape When the Victim is Male Versus Female. 1988 7p (Paper presented at the Western Psychological Association, 1988) (available from ERIC, No.ED299502)

Schult, Deborah and Schneider, Lawrence. Attribution of Blame toward Rape Victims. 1987 26p (Paper presented at the Southwestern Psychological Association, 1987) (available from ERIC, No.ED279953)

Travis, Shelley and Allgeier, Elizabeth. Attributions of Responsibility to Male and Female Victims of Rape and Robbery. 1986 17p (Paper presented at the Annual Meeting of the Midwestern Psychological Association, 1986) (available from ERIC, No. ED283064)

Williams, Joyce and Holmes, Karen. The Second Assault: Rape and Public Attitudes. Westport, CT: Greenwood Press, 1981

Witten, Barbara and Remer, Rory. Perceptions of Rape. 1985 19p (Paper presented at the American Educational Research Association, 1985) (available from ERIC, No.ED264473)

Yonker, Robert and others. Differences in College Students' Belief in Common Myths about Rape by Gender and Year in College. 1986 19p (available from ERIC, No.ED280332)

ATTITUDES ABOUT RAPE IN OUR SOCIETY

ARTICLES

Borden, Lynn and others. "Effects of a University Rape Prevention Program on Attitudes and Empathy Toward Rape", JOURNAL OF COLLEGE STUDENT DEVELOPMENT 29(2):132-136 March 1988

Briere, John and others. "Sexuality and Rape-Supportive Beliefs", INTERNATIONAL JOURNAL OF WOMEN'S STUDIES 8(4):398-403 September/October 1985

Brodt, Stephen. "'Rape Panic': Definition of a Crime Problem and Community Response", FREE INQUIRY IN CREATIVE SOCIOLOGY 15(2):183-187 November 1987

Burczyk, Katherine and Standing, Lionel. "Attitudes Towards Rape Victims: Effects of Victim Status, Sex of Victim, and Sex of Raper", SOCIAL BEHAVIOR AND PERSONALITY 17(1):1-8 1989

Claggett, Arthur. "Theoretical Consideration of Forcible Rape: A Critical Analysis", PSYCHOLOGY: A JOURNAL OF HUMAN BEHAVIOR 25(1):10-17 1988

Costin, Frank. "Beliefs about Rape and Women's Social Roles", ARCHIVES OF SEXUAL BEHAVIOR 14(4):319-325 August 1985

_____ and Schwarz, Norbert. "Beliefs about Rape and Women's Social Roles: A Four-Nation Study", JOURNAL OF INTERPERSONAL VIOLENCE 2(1):47-56 March 1987

Damrosch, S. "How Perceived Carelessness and Time of Attack Affect Nursing Students' Attributions about Rape Victims", PSYCHOLOGICAL REPORTS 56:531-536 April 1985

Deitz, S. and others. "Attribution of Responsibility for Rape: The Influence of Observer Empathy, Victim Resistance, and Victim Attractiveness", SEX ROLES 10:261-280 February 1984

di Maria, F. and di Nuovo, S. "Judgments of Aggression by Sicilian Observers", JOURNAL OF SOCIAL PSYCHOLOGY 126:187-196 April 1986

Edmonds, Ed and Cahoon, Delwin. "Attitudes Concerning Crimes Related to Clothing Worn by Female Victims", BULLETIN OF THE PSYCHONOMIC SOCIETY 24(6):444-446 November 1986

Fischer, Gloria. "College Student Attitudes Toward Forcible Date Rape: Changes after Taking a Human Sexuality Course", 12(1):42-46 Spring/Summer 1986

_____. "College Student Attitudes Toward Forcible Date Rape: I. Cognitive Predictors", ARCHIVES OF SEXUAL BEHAVIOR 15(6):457-466 December 1986

Freedman, Estelle. "'Uncontrolled Desires': The Response to the Sexual Psychopath, 1920-1960", JOURNAL OF AMERICAN HISTORY 74(1):83-106 June 1987

Garrett-Gooding, J. and Senter, F.. "Attitudes and Acts of Sexual Aggression on a University Campus", SOCIOLOGICAL INQUIRY 57:348-371 Fall 1987

Gerdes, Eugenia and others. "Perceptions of Rape Victims and Assailants: Effects of Physical Attractiveness, Acquaintance, and Subject Gender", SEX ROLES 19(3/4):141-153 August 1988

Giacopassi, David and Dull, Thomas. "Gender and Racial Differences in the Acceptance of Rape Myths within a College Population", SEX ROLES 15(1/2):63-75 July 1986

Gilmartin-Zena, Pat. "Attitudes about Rape Myths: Are Women's Studies Students Different?", FREE INQUIRY IN CREATIVE SOCIOLOGY 17(1):65-72 May 1989

_____. "Attitudes Toward Rape: Student Characteristics as Predictors", FREE INQUIRY IN CREATIVE SOCIOLOGY 15(2):175-182 November 1987

_____. "Gender Differences in Students' Attitudes Toward Rape", SOCIOLOGICAL FOCUS 21(4):279-292 October 1988

Hall, Eleanor and others. "Tolerance of Rape: A Sexist or Antisocial Attitude?", PSYCHOLOGY OF WOMEN QUARTERLY 10(2):101-117 June 1986

Hamlin, John. "Who's the Victim?: Women, Control, and Consciousness", WOMEN'S STUDIES INTERNATIONAL FORUM 11(3):223-233 1988

Harari, H. and others. "The Reaction to Rape by American Bystanders", JOURNAL OF SOCIAL PSYCHOLOGY 125:653-658 October 1985

Howard, Judith. "A Structural Approach to Sexual Attitudes: Interracial Patterns in Adolescents' Judgments about Sexual Intimacy", SOCIOLOGICAL PERSPECTIVES 31(1):88-121 January 1988

Howells, Kevin and others. "Perceptions of Rape in a British Sample: Effects of Relationship, Victim Status, Sex, and Attitudes to Women", BRITISH JOURNAL OF SOCIAL PSYCHOLOGY 23(1):35-40 February 1984

Jacobson, M. and Popovich, P. "Victim Attractiveness and Perceptions of Responsibility in an Ambiguous Rape Case", PSYCHOLOGY OF WOMEN QUARTERLY 8:100-104 Fall 1983

Janoff-Bulman, R. and others. "Cognitive Biases in Blaming the Victim", JOURNAL OF EXPERIMENTAL SOCIAL PSYCHOLOGY 21:161-177 March 1985

Karzua, J. and Carey, T. "Relative Preference and Adaptiveness of Behavioral Blame for Observers of Rape Victims", JOURNAL OF PERSONALITY 52:249-260 September 1984

Krahe, B. "Victim and Observer Characteristics as Determinants of Responsibility Attributions to Victims of Rape", JOURNAL OF APPLIED SOCIAL PSYCHOLOGY 18:50-58 January 1988

Larsen, Knud and Long, Ed. "Attitudes toward Rape", JOURNAL OF SEX RESEARCH 24:299-304 1988

LeDoux, John and Hazelwood, Robert. "Police Attitudes and Beliefs Toward Rape", JOURNAL OF POLICE SCIENCE AND ADMINISTRATION 13(3):211-220 September 1985

Linz, D. "Exposure to Sexually Explicit Materials and Attitudes Toward Rape: A Comparison of Study Results", JOURNAL OF SEX RESEARCH 26:50-84 February 1989

Macrae, Neil and Shepherd, John. "Sex Differences in the Perception of Rape Victims", JOURNAL OF INTERPERSONAL VIOLENCE 4(3):278-288 September 1989

Margalin, Leslie and others. "When a Kiss Is Not Just a Kiss: Relating Violations of Consent in Kissing to Rape Myth Acceptance", SEX ROLES 20:231-243 March 1989

Marolla, Joseph and Scully, Diana. "Attitudes Toward Women, Violence, and Rape: A Comparison of Convicted Rapists and Other Felons", DEVIANT BEHAVIOR 7(4):337-355 1986

Mayerson, Suzin and Taylor, Dalmas. "The Effects of Rape Myth Pornography on Women's Attitudes and the Mediating Role of Sex Role Stereotyping", SEX ROLES 17(5/6):321-338 September 1987

Muehlenhard, Charlene. "'Nice Women' Don't Say Yes and 'Real Men' Don't Say No: How Miscommunication and the Double Standard Can Cause Sexual Problems", WOMEN AND THERAPY 7(2/3):95-108 1988

_____ **and MacNaughton, Jennifer.** "Women's Beliefs about Women Who 'Lead Men On'", JOURNAL OF SOCIAL AND CLINICAL PSYCHOLOGY 7(1):65-79 1988

Orcutt, James and Faison, Rebecca. "Sex-Role Attitude Change and Reporting of Rape Victimization, 1973-1985", SOCIOLOGICAL QUARTERLY 29(4):589-604 December 1988

Peterson, Dena and Pfost, Karen. "Influence of Rock Videos on Attitudes of Violence Against Women", PSYCHOLOGICAL REPORTS 64(1):319-322 February 1989

Remer, Rory and Witten, Barbara. "Conceptions of Rape", VIOLENCE AND VICTIMS 3(3):217-232 Fall 1988

Ryan, Kathryn. "Rape and Seduction Scripts", PSYCHOLOGY OF WOMEN QUARTERLY 12:237-245 June 1988

Sattem, Linda and others. "Sex-Role Stereotypes and Commitment of Rape", SEX ROLES 11(9/10):849-860 November 1984

Smith, Ronald and others. "Social Cognitions about Adult Male Victims of Female Sexual Assault", JOURNAL OF SEX RESEARCH 24:101-112 1988

Spees, Emil. "College Students' Sexual Attitudes and Behaviors, 1974-1985: A Review of the Literature", JOURNAL OF COLLEGE STUDENT PERSONNEL 28(2):135-140 March 1987

Walsh, A. "Gender-Based Differences: A Study of Probation Officers' Attitudes about, and Recommendations for, Felony Sexual Assault Cases", CRIMINOLOGY 22:371-387 August 1984

Ward, Colleen. "The Attitudes Toward Rape Victims Scale: Construction, Validation and Cross-Cultural Applicability", PSYCHOLOGY OF WOMEN QUARTERLY 12(2):127-146 1988

Williams, Joyce. "Mexican American and Anglo Attitudes about Sex Roles and Rape", FREE INQUIRY IN CREATIVE SOCIOLOGY 13(1):15-20 May 1985

_____. "Secondary Victimization: Confronting Public Attitudes About Rape", VICTIMOLOGY 9(1):66-81 1984

Winkel, Fraus. "Changing Misconceptions about Rape Through Informational Campaigns: A Model", VICTIMOLOGY 9(2):262-272 1984

Wyer, Robert and others. "Cognitive Mediators of Reactions to Rape", JOURNAL OF PERSONALITY AND SOCIAL PSYCHOLOGY 48:324-338 February 1985

RACE AND CLASS ASPECTS

BOOKS, PAMPHLETS

Burns, Maryviolet, ed. The Speaking Profits Us: Violence in the Lives of Women of Color. Seattle, WA: Center for the Prevention of Sexual and Domestic Violence, 1986

Lee, Kristine and Woo, Linda. Rape is an Asian Problem, Too. Seattle, WA: Seattle Rape Relief, 1987

Schwendinger, Julia and Schwendinger, Herman. Rape and Inequality. Beverly Hills, CA: Sage Publications, 1983

Villa Romo, Velma. Rape in the Barrio. Santa Barbara, CA: The Author, 1978 38p

Williams, Linda. Race and Rape: The Black Woman as Legitimate Victim. 1986 36p (Research sponsored by the United States, Department of Health and Human Services, National Institute of Mental Health) (available from ERIC, No. ED284870)

RACE AND CLASS ASPECTS

ARTICLES

Bogira, Steve. "Right to Be Safe: Black Rape Victims and the Police", IN THESE TIMES 10(15):12+ March 12-18, 1986

Bumiller, Kristin. "Rape as a Legal Symbol: An Essay on Sexual Violence and Racism", UNIVERSITY OF MIAMI LAW REVIEW 42:75-91 1987

Davis, Angela. "Rape, Racism and the Capitalist Setting", BLACK SCHOLAR 9(7):24-30 1978

Field, Hubert. "Rape Trials and Jurors' Decisions: A Psycholegal Analysis of the Effects of Victim, Defendant, and Case Characteristics", LAW AND HUMAN BEHAVIOR 3(4):261-284 1979

Fischer, Gloria. "Hispanic and Majority Student Attitudes Toward Forcible Date Rape as a Function of Differences in Attitudes Toward Women", SEX ROLES 17(1/2):93-101 July 1987

Giacopassi, David and Dull, Thomas. "Gender and Racial Differences in the Acceptance of Rape Myths within a College Population", SEX ROLES 15(1/2):63-75 July 1986

Hamilton, Jean. "Emotional Consequences of Victimization and Discrimination in 'Special Populations' of Women", PSYCHIATRIC CLINICS OF NORTH AMERICA 12(1):35-51 March 1989

Heilbrun, Alfred and Cross, John. "An Analysis of Rape Patterns in White and Black Rapists", JOURNAL OF SOCIAL PSYCHOLOGY 108(1):83-87 June 1979

Hine, Darlene. "Rape and the Inner Lives of Black Women in the Middle West", SIGNS 14:900+ Summer 1989

Howard, Judith. "A Structural Approach to Sexual Attitudes: Interracial Patterns of Adolescents' Judgments about Sexual Intimacy", SOCIOLOGICAL PERSPECTIVES 31(1):88-121 January 1988

Kirk, Stuart. "The Sex Offenses of Blacks and Whites", ARCHIVES OF SEXUAL BEHAVIOR 4(3):295-302 May 1975

Klein, Kitty and Creech, Blanche. "Race, Rape, and Bias: Distortion of Prior Odds and Meaning Changes", BASIC AND APPLIED SOCIAL PSYCHOLOGY 3(1):21-33 March 1982 (two experiments investigated how racial bias affects juror decision making)

LaFree, Gary. "Male Power and Female Victimization: Toward a Theory of Interracial Rape", AMERICAN JOURNAL OF SOCIOLOGY 88(2):311-328 September 1982

LeBeau, James. "Is Interracial Rape Different?", SOCIOLOGY AND SOCIAL RESEARCH 73(1):43-46 October 1988

_____. "Rape and Racial Patterns", JOURNAL OF OFFENDER COUNSELING, SERVICES AND REHABILITATION 9(1/2):125-148 Fall/Winter 1984

Maume, David, Jr. "Inequality and Metropolitan Rape Rates: A Routine Activity", JUSTICE QUARTERLY 6(4):513-528 1989

Miller, Marina and Hewitt, Jay. "Conviction of a Defendant as a Function of Juror-Victim Racial Similarity", JOURNAL OF SOCIAL PSYCHOLOGY 105(1):159-160 June 1978

O'Brien, Robert. "The Interracial Nature of Violent Crimes: A Re-examination", AMERICAN JOURNAL OF SOCIOLOGY 92(4):817-835 January 1987

Omolade, B. "Black Women, Black Men And Tawana Brawley: The Shared Condition", HARVARD WOMEN'S LAW JOURNAL 12:11-23 Spring 1989

Pavich, Emma. "A Chicana Perspective on Mexican Culture and Sexuality", JOURNAL OF SOCIAL WORK AND HUMAN SEXUALITY 4(3):47-65 Spring 1986

Peterson, Ruth and Bailey, William. "Forcible Rape, Poverty, and Economic Inequality in U.S. Metropolitan Communities", JOURNAL OF QUANTITATIVE CRIMINOLOGY 4(2):99-119 June 1988

Robkin, J. "The Epidemiology of Forcible Rape", AMERICAN JOURNAL OF ORTHOPSYCHIATRY 49(4):634-647 1979

Smith, M. and Bennett, Nathan. "Poverty, Inequality, and Theories of Forcible Rape", CRIME AND DELINQUENCY 31(2):295-305 April 1985

Uqwueqbu, Denis. "Black Jurors' Personality Trait Attribution to a Rape Case Defendant", SOCIAL BEHAVIOR AND PERSONALITY 4(2):193-201 1976

_____. "Racial and Evidential Factors in Juror Attribution of Legal Responsibility", JOURNAL OF EXPERIMENTAL SOCIAL PSYCHOLOGY 15(2):133-146 March 1979

Williams, Joyce and Holmes, Karen. "In Judgment of Victims: The Social Context of Rape", JOURNAL OF SOCIOLOGY AND SOCIAL WELFARE 9(1):154-169 March 1982 (examines the linkages between 3 racial/ethnic groups)

BOOKS, PAMPHLETS

Ellis, Lee. Theories of Rape: Inquiries into the Causes of Sexual Aggression. New York: Hemisphere Publishing, 1989

Flowers, R. Violent Women: Are They Catching Up to Violent Men or Have They Surpassed Them? 1987 19p (includes section entitled "The Female Rapist") (available from ERIC, No.ED301496)

Groth, A. Men Who Rape: The Psychology of the Offender. New York: Plenum Press, 1979

Levine, Sylvia and Koenig, Joseph, eds. Why Men Rape: Interviews with Convicted Rapists. London: W.H. Allen, 1982

Otey, Emeline and Ryan, Gail, eds. Adolescent Sex Offenders: Issues in Research and Treatment. 1985 (Research sponsored by the United States, Department of Health and Human Services, National Center for the Control and Prevention of Rape) (available from ERIC, No.ED275930)

Prentky, Robert and Quinsey, Vernon, eds. Human Sexual Aggression: Current Perspectives. New York: New York Academy of Sciences, 1988

Rada, Richard, ed. Clinical Aspects of the Rapist. New York: Grune and Stratton, 1978

Scully, Diana. Understanding Sexual Violence: A Study of Convicted Rapists. Cambridge, MA: Unwin Hyman, 1990

West, Donald and others. Understanding Sexual Attacks: A Study Based Upon a Group of Rapists undergoing Psychotherapy. London: Heinemann Educational, 1978

ARTICLES

Alder, Christine. "The Convicted Rapist: A Sexual or a Violent Offender?", CRIMINAL JUSTICE AND BEHAVIOR 11:157-178 June 1984
_____. "An Exploration of Self-Reported Sexually Aggressive Behavior", CRIME AND DELINQUENCY 31(2):306-331 April 1985
Annis, Lawrence and others. "Victim Workers as Therapists for Incarcerated Sex Offenders", VICTIMOLOGY 9(3/4):426-435 1984
Bard, Leonard and others. "A Descriptive Study of Rapists and Child Molesters: Developmental, Clinical, and Criminal Characteristics", BEHAVIORAL SCIENCES AND THE LAW 5(2):203-220 Spring 1987
Berlin, Fred. "Interviews with 5 Rapists", AMERICAN JOURNAL OF FORENSIC PSYCHOLOGY 5(2):3-33 1987
Burnam, M. and others. "Sexual Assault and Mental Disorders in a Community Population", JOURNAL OF CONSULTING AND CLINICAL PSYCHOLOGY 56:843-850 December 1988
Coodley, Alfred. "Psychodynamics of Rapists", AMERICAN JOURNAL OF FORENSIC PSYCHIATRY 6(2):38-47 1985
Corder, Bilie and others. "Characteristics of Two Types of Juvenile Rapists: Implications for Treatment and Prediction", JOURNAL OF OFFENDER COUNSELING 7(1):10-17 October 1986
Earls, C. and Proulx, J. "The Differentiation of Francophone Rapists and Nonrapists Using Penile Circumferential Measures", CRIMINAL JUSTICE AND BEHAVIOR 13:419-429 December 1986
Freund, Kurt and others. "Males Disposed to Commit Rape", ARCHIVES OF SEXUAL BEHAVIOR 15(1):23-35 February 1986
Glasman, C. "Discussing Rape with Rapists -- Or Can Men Change?", NEW LAW JOURNAL 139:969-970 July 14, 1989
Grier, Priscilla. "Cognitive Problem-Solving Skills in Antisocial Rapists", CRIMINAL JUSTICE AND BEHAVIOR 15(4):501-514 December 1988
Hamilton, M. and Yee, J. "Rape Knowledge and Propensity to Rape", JOURNAL OF RESEARCH IN PERSONALITY 24(1):111-122 March 1990
Hazelwood, Robert and Burgess, A. "An Introduction to the Serial Rapist: Research by the FBI", FBI LAW ENFORCEMENT BULLETIN 56:16-24 September 1987
_____ and Warren, J. "The Serial Rapist: His Characteristics and Victims", FBI LAW ENFORCEMENT BULLETIN 58:10-17 January 1989; 58:18-25 February 1989

_____ **and others.** "Serial Rape: Correlates of Increased Aggression and the Relationship of Offender Pleasure to Victim Resistance", JOURNAL OF INTERPERSONAL VIOLENCE 4(1):65-78 March 1989

Kalichman, S. and others. "Cluster Analytically Derived MMPI Profile Subgroups of Incarcerated Adult Rapists", JOURNAL OF CLINICAL PSYCHOLOGY 45(1):149-155 January 1989

Kanin, Eugene. "Date Rapists: Differential Sexual Socialization and Relative Deprivation", ARCHIVES OF SEXUAL BEHAVIOR 14(3):219-231 June 1985

Kavoussi, R. "Psychiatric Diagnoses in Adolescent Sex Offenders", JOURNAL OF THE AMERICAN ACADEMY OF CHILD AND ADOLESCENT PSYCHIATRY 27:241-243 March 1988

Knight, Raymond and Prentky, Robert. "The Developmental Antecedents and Adult Adaptations of Rapist Subtypes", CRIMINAL JUSTICE AND BEHAVIOR 14(4):403-426 December 1987

Koss, Mary and others. "Nonstranger Sexual Aggression: A Discriminant Analysis of the Psychological Characteristics of Undetected Offenders", SEX ROLES 12:981-992 May 1985

Kruttschnitt, C. "A Sociological, Offender-Based Study of Rape", SOCIOLOGICAL QUARTERLY 30:305-329 Summer 1989

Ladouceur, Patricia and Temple, Mark. "Substance Use among Rapists: A Comparison with Other Serious Felons", CRIME AND DELINQUENCY 31(2):269-294 April 1985

LeBeau, James. "The Journey to Rape: Geographic Distance and the Rapist's Method of Approaching the Victim", JOURNAL OF POLICE SCIENCE AND ADMINISTRATION 15(2):129-136 June 1987

Levin, Saul and Stava, Lawrence. "Personality Characteristics of Sex Offenders: A Review", ARCHIVES OF SEXUAL BEHAVIOR 16(1):57-79 February 1987

Lipton, David and others. "Heterosocial Perception in Rapists", JOURNAL OF CONSULTING AND CLINICAL PSYCHOLOGY 55(1):17-21 February 1987

Lisak, D. and Roth, S. "Motivational Factors in Nonincarcerated Sexually Aggressive Men", JOURNAL OF PERSONALITY AND SOCIAL PSYCHOLOGY 55:795-802 November 1988

Lizotte, Alan. "Determinants of Completing Rape and Assault", JOURNAL OF QUANTITATIVE CRIMINOLOGY 2(3):203-217 September 1986

Malamuth, Neil. "The Attraction to Sexual Aggression Scale: I", JOURNAL OF SEX RESEARCH 26(1):26-49 February 1989

Marolla, Joseph and Scully, Diana. "Attitudes Toward Women, Violence, and Rape: A Comparison of Convicted Rapists and Other Felons", DEVIANT BEHAVIOR 7(4):337-355 1986

Marshall, W. "The Use of Sexually Explicit Stimuli by Rapists, Child Molesters, and Nonoffenders", JOURNAL OF SEX RESEARCH 25:267-288 May 1988

Overholser, James and Beck, Steven. "The Classification of Rapists and Child Molesters", JOURNAL OF OFFENDER COUNSELING 13(1):15-25 1988

_____ and Beck, Steven. "Multimethod Assessment of Rapists, Child Molesters, and Three Control Groups on Behavioral and Psychological Measures", JOURNAL OF CONSULTING AND CLINICAL PSYCHOLOGY 54:682-687 October 1986

Palmer, Craig. "Twelve Reasons Why Rape Is Not Sexually Motivated: A Skeptical Examination", JOURNAL OF SEX RESEARCH 25(4):512-530 November 1988

Peterson, Ruth and Bailey, William. "Forcible Rape, Poverty, and Economic Inequality in U.S. Metropolitan Communities", JOURNAL OF QUANTITATIVE CRIMINOLOGY 4(2):99-119 June 1988

Petrovich, M. and Templer, D. "Heterosexual Molestation of Children Who Later Become Rapists", PSYCHOLOGICAL REPORTS 54:810 June 1984

Prentky, R. and Knight, R. "Impulsivity in the Lifestyle and Criminal Behavior of Sexual Offenders", CRIMINAL JUSTICE AND BEHAVIOR 13:141-164 June 1986

Quinsey, V. and others. "Sexual Arousal to Nonsexual Violence and Sadomasochistic Themes among Rapists and Non-Sex-Offenders", JOURNAL OF CONSULTING AND CLINICAL PSYCHOLOGY 52:651-657 August 1984

Rapaport, K. and Burkhart, B. "Personality and Attitudinal Characteristics of Sexually Coercive College Males", JOURNAL OF ABNORMAL PSYCHOLOGY 93:216-221 May 1984

Ressler, Robert and others. "Murders Who Rape and Mutilate", JOURNAL OF INTERPERSONAL VIOLENCE 1(3):273-287 September 1986

Sattem, Linda and others. "Sex Role Stereotypes and Commitment of Rape", SEX ROLES 11:849-860 November 1984

Scott, Ronald and Tetreault, Laurie. "Attitudes of Rapists and Other Violent Offenders Toward Women", JOURNAL OF SOCIAL PSYCHOLOGY 127(4):375-380 August 1987

Scully, Diana. "Convicted Rapists' Perceptions of Self and Victim: Role Taking and Emotions", GENDER AND SOCIETY 2(2):200-213 June 1988

_____ and Marolla, Joseph. "Convicted Rapists' Vocabulary of Motive: Excuses and Justifications", SOCIAL PROBLEMS 31(5):530-544 June 1984

_____ and Marolla, Joseph. "'Riding the Bull at Gilley's': Convicted Rapists Describe the Rewards of Rape", SOCIAL PROBLEMS 32(3):251-263 February 1985

Segal, Z. and Marshall, W. "Heterosexual Social Skills in a Population of Rapists and Child Molesters", JOURNAL OF CONSULTING CLINICAL PSYCHOLOGY 53:55-63 Fall 1985

Seghorn, T. and others. "Childhood Sexual Abuse in the Lives of Sexually Aggressive Offenders", JOURNAL OF THE AMERICAN ACADEMY OF CHILD AND ADOLESCENT PSYCHIATRY 26:262-267 March 1987

Stermac, Lana and Quinsey, Vernon. "Social Competence among Rapists", BEHAVIORAL ASSESSMENT 8(2):171-185 Spring 1986

Tetreault, Scott and Tetreault, Laurie. "Attitudes of Rapists and Other Violent Offenders Toward Women", JOURNAL OF SOCIAL PSYCHOLOGY 127(4):375-380 1987

Tingle, D. and others. "Childhood and Adolescent Characteristics of Pedophiles and Rapists", INTERNATIONAL JOURNAL OF LAW AND PSYCHIATRY 9:103-116 1986

Van Ness, Shela. "Rape as Instrumental Violence: A Study of Youth Offenders", JOURNAL OF OFFENDER COUNSELING, SERVICES AND REHABILITATION 9(1/2):161-170 Fall/Winter 1984

Vinogradov, Sophia and others. "Patterns of Behavior in Adolescent Rape", AMERICAN JOURNAL OF ORTHOPSYCHIATRY 58(2):179-187 April 1988

Wiener, Richard and Rinehart, Nora. "Psychological Causality in the Attribution of Responsibility for Rape", SEX ROLES 14(7/8):369-382 1986

Yourell, Asha and McCabe, Marita. "The Motivations Underlying Male Rape of Women", AUSTRALIAN JOURNAL OF SEX, MARRIAGE AND FAMILY 9(4):215-224 November 1988

PORNOGRAPHY AND RAPE

BOOKS, PAMPHLETS AND PAPERS

Baron, L. and Straus, M. Rape and Its Relation to Social Disorganization, Pornography and Sexual Inequality. (Paper presented at the International Congress on Rape, Israel, April 1986)

Burgess, A., ed. Handbook of Research on Pornography and Sexual Assault. New York: Garland, 1984

Carter, D. and others, eds. Pornography, Social Science, Legal and Clinical Perspectives. New York: Women Against Pornography, [nd]

Donnerstein, Edward and others. The Question of Pornography: Research Findings and Policy Implications. New York: Free Press, 1987

Gray, Susan. Pornography and Violence Against Women: Is There Hard Evidence on Hard Core? (Paper presented at the annual meeting of the Eastern Sociological Society, New York, March 1981)

Malamuth, Neil and Donnerstein, Edward, eds. Pornography and Sexual Aggression. Orlando, FL: Academic Press, 1984

_____ **and others.** Exposure to Pornography and Reaction to Rape. (Paper presented at the 86th annual convention of the American Psychological Association, New York, 1979)

Nelson, E. The Influence of Pornography on Behavior. London: Academic Press, 1982

Social Science Studies on Pornography and Aggression. New York: Women Against Pornography, [nd] (literature packet)

Yaffe, Maurice and Nelson, Edward, eds. The Influence of Pornography on Behavior. New York: Academic Press, 1982

ARTICLES

Ashley, Barbara and Ashley, David. "Sex as Violence: The Body Against Intimacy", INTERNATIONAL JOURNAL OF WOMEN'S STUDIES 7:352-371 September/October 1984

Baron, Larry. "Immoral, Inviolate or Inconclusive?", SOCIETY 24:6-12 July/August 1987

Baron, R. and Bell, P. "Sexual Arousal and Aggression by Males: Effects of Type of Erotic Stimuli and Prior Provocation", JOURNAL OF PERSONALITY AND SOCIAL PSYCHOLOGY 35:79-87 1977

_____ **and Straus, M.** "Sexual Stratification, Pornography and Rape", in Malamuth, Neil and Donnerstein, Edward, eds. Pornography and Sexual Aggression. Orlando, FL: Academic Press, 1984

Brannigan, Augustine. "Is Obscenity Criminogenic?", SOCIETY 24:12-19 July/August 1987

_____ **and Kapardis, Andros.** "The Controversy over Pornography and Sex Crimes: The Criminological Evidence and Beyond", AUSTRALIAN AND NEW ZEALAND JOURNAL OF CRIMINOLOGY 19:259-284 December 1986

_____ **and others.** "Pornography and Behavior: Alternative Explanations", JOURNAL OF COMMUNICATION 37(3):185-192 Summer 1987

Carter, Daniel and others. "Use of Pornography in the Criminal and Developmental Histories of Sexual Offenders", JOURNAL OF INTERPERSONAL VIOLENCE 2(2):196-211 June 1987

Cenite, J. and Malamuth, Neil. "Effects of Repeated Exposure to Sexually Violent or Non-Violent Stimuli on Sexual Arousal to Rape and Nonrape Depictions", BEHAVIOR RESEARCH AND THERAPY 22(5):535-548 1984

Check, James and Malamuth, Neil. "Pornography and Sexual Aggression: A Social Learning Theory Analysis", in McLaughlin, M., ed. Communication Yearbooks, Volume 9. Beverly Hills, CA: Sage Publications, 1985

_____ **and Malamuth, Neil.** "Violent Pornography, Feminism and Social Learning Theory", AGGRESSIVE BEHAVIOR 9:106-107 1983

Court, J. "Pornography and Sex Crimes: A Re-Evaluation in Light of Recent Trends Around the World", INTERNATIONAL JOURNAL OF CRIMINOLOGY AND PENOLOGY 5:129-157 1977

_____ . "Sex and Violence: A Ripple Effect", in Malamuth, Neil and Donnerstein, Edward, eds. Pornography and Sexual Aggression. Orlando, FL: Academic Press, 1984

Demare, Dano and others. "Violent Pornography and Self-Reported Likelihood of Sexual Aggression", JOURNAL OF RESEARCH IN PERSONALITY 22(2):140-153 June 1988

Dienstbier, R. "Sex and Violence: Can Research Have It Both Ways?", JOURNAL OF COMMUNICATION 27:176-188 1977

Donnerstein, Edward. "Aggressive Erotica and Violence Against Women", JOURNAL OF PERSONALITY AND SOCIAL PSYCHOLOGY 39:269-277 1980

_____. "Aggressive Pornography: Can It Influence Aggression Against Women?", in Albee, G. and others, eds. Promoting Sexual Responsibility and Preventing Sexual Problems. Hanover, NH: University of New England Press, 1983

_____. "Erotica and Human Aggression", in Geen, R. and Donnerstein, Edward, eds. Aggression: Theoretical and Empirical Reviews, Volume 2. New York: Academic Press, 1983

_____. "Pornography and Violence Against Women", ANNALS OF THE NEW YORK ACADEMY OF SCIENCES 347:277-288 1980

_____. "Pornography: Its Effect on Violence Against Women", in Malamuth, Neil and Donnerstein, Edward, eds. Pornography and Sexual Aggression. Orlando, FL: Academic Press, 1984

_____ and Barrett, G. "The Effects of Erotic Stimuli on Male Aggression Toward Females", JOURNAL OF PERSONALITY AND SOCIAL PSYCHOLOGY 36:180-188 1978

_____ and Berkowitz, Leonard. "Victim Reactions in Aggressive Erotic Films as a Factor in Violence Against Women", JOURNAL OF PERSONALITY AND SOCIAL PSYCHOLOGY 41(4):710-724 1981

Mould, Douglas. "A Critical Analysis of Recent Research on Violent Erotica", JOURNAL OF SEX RESEARCH 24:326-340 1988

Donnerstein, Edward and Linz, Daniel. "A Critical Analysis of "A Critical Analysis of Recent Research on Violent Erotica"", JOURNAL OF SEX RESEARCH 24:348-352 1988

_____ and Hallam, J. "The Facilitating Effects of Erotica on Aggression Towards Females", JOURNAL OF PERSONALITY AND SOCIAL PSYCHOLOGY 36:1270-1277 1978

_____ and Linz, Daniel. "Mass Media Sexual Violence and Male Viewers: Current Theory and Research", AMERICAN BEHAVIORAL SCIENTIST 29(5):601-618 May/June 1986

_____ and Linz, Daniel. "The Question of Pornography", PSYCHOLOGY TODAY 20(12):56-59 December 1986

_____ and Linz, Daniel. "Sexual Violence in the Media: A Warning", PSYCHOLOGY TODAY January 1984, p14-15

_____ and others. "Erotic Stimuli and Aggression: Facilitation or Inhibition", JOURNAL OF PERSONALITY AND SOCIAL PSYCHOLOGY 32:237-244 1975

Garcia, Luis. "Exposure to Pornography and Attitudes about Women and Rape: A Correlational Study", JOURNAL OF SEX RESEARCH 22(3):378-385 August 1986

Goldstein, M. and others. "Exposure to Pornography and Sexual Behavior in Deviant and Normal Groups", in Technical Report of the Commission on Obscenity and Pornography, Volume 7. Washington, DC: Government Printing Office, 1970, p1-90

Gray, Susan. "Exposure to Pornography and Aggression Toward Women: The Case of The Angry Male", SOCIAL PROBLEMS 29(4):387-398 April 1982

Howard, J. and others. "Effects of Exposure to Pornography", in Technical Report of the Commission on Obscenity and Pornography, Volume 8. Washington, DC: Government Printing Office, 1970, p97-132

Jaffee, David and Straus, Murray. "Sexual Climate and Reported Rape: A State-Level Analysis", ARCHIVES OF SEXUAL BEHAVIOR 16(2):107-123 April 1987

Kutchinsky, B. "The Effect of Easy Availability of Pornography on the Incidence of Sex Crimes: The Danish Experience", JOURNAL OF SOCIAL ISSUES 29(3):163-181

_____. "The Effect of Pornography: A Pilot Experiment on Perception, Behavior and Attitudes", in Technical Report of the Commission on Obscenity and Pornography, Volume 8. Washington, DC: Government Printing Office, 1970, p133-169

Leonard, Kenneth and Taylor, Stuart. "Exposure to Pornography, Permissive and Nonpermissive Cues, and Male Aggression Toward Females", MOTIVATION AND EMOTION 7(3):291-299 September 1983

Linz, Daniel. "The Effects of Multiple Exposures to Filmed Violence Against Women", JOURNAL OF COMMUNICATION 34(3):130-147 Summer 1984

_____. "Exposure to Sexually Explicit Materials and Attitudes Toward Rape: A Comparison of Study Results", JOURNAL OF SEX RESEARCH 26(1):50-84 February 1989

_____ and others. "Colloquy: The Methods and Merits of Pornography Research", JOURNAL OF COMMUNICATION 38(2):180-192 Spring 1988

_____ and others. "Effects of Long-Term Exposure to Violent and Sexually Degrading Depictions of Women", JOURNAL OF PERSONALITY AND SOCIAL PSYCHOLOGY 55(5):758-768 November 1988

MacKinnon, C. "Sexuality, Pornography, and Method: 'Pleasure under Patriarchy'", ETHICS 99:314-346 January 1989

Malamuth, Neil. "The Mass Media and Aggression Against Women: Research Findings and Prevention", in Burgess, A., ed. Handbook of Research on Pornography and Sexual Assault. New York: Garland Publishers, 1984

_____. "Rape Fantasies as a Function of Exposure to Violent-Sexual Stimuli", ARCHIVES OF SEXUAL BEHAVIOR 10:33-47 1981

_____ and Briere, John. "Sexual Violence in the Media: Indirect Effects on Aggression Against Women", JOURNAL OF SOCIAL ISSUES 42(3):75-92 1986

_____ and Ceniti, Joseph. "Repeated Exposure to Violent and Nonviolent Pornography: Likelihood of Raping Ratings and Laboratory Aggression Against Women", AGGRESSIVE BEHAVIOR 12(2):129-137 1986

_____ and Check, James. "The Effects of Aggressive Pornography on Beliefs in Rape Myths: Individual Differences", JOURNAL OF RESEARCH IN PERSONALITY 19(3):299-320 September 1985

Mould, Douglas. "A Critical Analysis of Recent Research on Violent Erotica", JOURNAL OF SEX RESEARCH 24:326-340 1988

Malamuth, Neil. "Research on 'Violent Erotica': A Reply", JOURNAL OF SEX RESEARCH 24:340-348 1988

Mould, Douglas. "A Critical Analysis of 'A Critical Analysis of Recent Literature on Violent Erotica': A Reply to Malamuth and Donnerstein and Linz", JOURNAL OF SEX RESEARCH 24:353-358 1988

_____ and Check, James. "The Effects of Mass Media Exposure on Acceptance of Violence Against Women: A Field Experiment", JOURNAL OF RESEARCH IN PERSONALITY 15:436-446 1981

_____ and Donnerstein, Edward. "The Effects of Aggressive-Pornographic Mass Media Stimuli", in Berkowitz, Leonard, ed. Advances in Experimental Social Psychology, Volume 15. New York: Academic Press, 1982, p103-124

_____ and others. "Sexual Arousal and Aggression: Recent Experiments and Theoretical Issues", JOURNAL OF SOCIAL ISSUES 33:110-133 1977

Masterson, John. "The Effects of Erotica and Pornography on Attitudes and Behavior: A Review", BULLETIN OF THE BRITISH PSYCHOLOGY SOCIETY 37:249-252 August 1984

Mayerson, Suzin and Taylor, Dalmas. "The Effects of Rape Myth Pornography on Women's Attitudes and the Mediating Role of Sex Role Stereotyping", SEX ROLES 17(5/6):321-338 September 1987

McCormack, Thelma. "Making Sense of Research on Pornography", in Burstyn, V., ed. Women Against Censorship. Toronto: Douglas and McIntyre, 1985

Meyer, T. "The Effects of Sexually Arousing and Violent Films on Aggressive Behavior", JOURNAL OF SEX RESEARCH 8:324-333 1972

Palys, T. "Testing the Common Wisdom: The Social Content of Video Pornography", CANADIAN PSYCHOLOGY 27(1):22-35 January 1986

Pfaus, James and others. "Soundtrack Contents and Depicted Sexual Violence", ARCHIVES OF SEXUAL BEHAVIOR 15(3):231-237 June 1986

Russell, Diana. "Pornography and Rape: A Causal Model", POLITICAL PSYCHOLOGY 9(1):41-73 March 1988

Scott, Joseph and Schwalm, Loretta. "Rape Rates and the Circulation Rates of Adult Magazines", JOURNAL OF SEX RESEARCH 24:241-250 1988

Sharp, Imogen. "Pornography and Sex-Related Crime: A Sociological Perspective", BULLETIN OF THE HONG KONG PSYCHOLOGICAL SOCIETY 16/17:73-81 January/July 1986

Silbert, Mimi and Pines, Ayala. "Pornography and Sexual Abuse of Women", SEX ROLES 10(11/12):857-868 June 1984

Smeaton, George and Byrne, Donn. "The Effects of R-Rated Violence and Erotica: Individual Differences, and Victim Characteristics on Acquaintance Rape Proclivity", JOURNAL OF RESEARCH IN PERSONALITY 21(2):171-184 June 1987

Tong, Rosemarie. "Women, Pornography, and the Law", ACADEME 73(5):14-22 September/October 1987

Walker, C. "Erotic Stimuli and the Aggressive Sexual Offender", in Technical Report of the Commission on Obscenity and Pornography, Volume 7. Washington, DC: Government Printing Office, 1970, p91-147

Wilson, W. "Can Pornography Contribute to the Prevention of Sexual Problems", in Qualls, C. and others, eds. The Prevention of Sexual Disorders: Issues and Approaches. New York: Plenum Press, 1978

Zillman, Dolf and Bryant, Jennings. "Effects of Massive Exposure to Pornography", in Malamuth, Neil and Donnerstein, Edward, eds. Pornography and Sexual Aggression. New York: Academic Press, 1984

_____ **and Bryant, Jennings.** "Pornography, Sexual Callousness, and the Trivialization of Rape", JOURNAL OF COMMUNICATION 32:10-21 Autumn 1982

Christensen, Ferrel. "Sexual Callousness Re-Examined", JOURNAL OF COMMUNICATION 36:174-188 Winter 1986

Discussion. JOURNAL OF COMMUNICATION 38:180-192 Spring 1988

Zillman, Dolf and Bryant, Jennings. "'Sexual Callousness Re-examined': Reply", JOURNAL OF COMMUNICATION 36(1):184-188 Winter 1986

Gross, Larry. "Pornography and Social Science Research: Some Questions....", JOURNAL OF COMMUNICATION 33(4):107-111 Fall 1983

Zillman, Dolf and Bryant, Jennings. "Pornography and Social Science Research: ...Higher Moralities", JOURNAL OF COMMUNICATION 33(4):111-114 Fall 1983

Brannigan, Augustine and others. "Pornography and Behavior: Alternative Explanations", JOURNAL OF COMMUNICATION 37(3):185-192 Summer 1987

_____ **and Bryant, Jennings.** "'Pornography and Behavior: Alternative Explanations': Reply", JOURNAL OF COMMUNICATION 37(3):189-192 Summer 1987

BOOKS, DOCUMENTS, PAMPHLETS

Adams, Caren and others. No Is not Enough: Helping Teenagers Avoid Sexual Assault. San Luis Obispo, CA: Impact Publishers, 1984

Bart, Pauline and O'Brien, Patricia. Stopping Rape: Successful Survival Strategies. New York: Pergamon Press, 1985

Booher, Dianna. Rape: What Would You Do If...?. New York: J. Messner, 1981

Burgess, Ann, ed. Rape and Sexual Assault. New York: Garland Publishing, 1985

Dean, Charles and deBruyn-Kops, Mary. The Crime and the Consequences of Rape. Springfield, IL: Thomas, 1982

Fein, Judith. Are You a Target?: A Guide to Self-Protection, Personal Safety, and Rape Prevention. San Francisco, CA: Torrance Publishing, 1988

Green, R. Rape: The New Attitude for Prevention. Torrance, CA: Green Productions, 1986 89p

Kaufman, Doris and others. Safe Within Yourself: A Woman's Guide to Rape Prevention and Self-Defense. Alexandria, VA: Visage Press, 1980

Keller, Daniel. The Prevention of Rape and Sexual Assault on Campus. Goshen, KY: Campus Crime Prevention Programs, 1989 97p

Krebill, Joan and Taylor, Julie. A Teaching Guide to Preventing Adolescent Sexual Abuse. Santa Cruz, CA: Network Publications, 1988

Landino, Rita and Moynihan, Barbara. The New Haven College Consortium on Sexual Assault: A Collaborative Model. 1987 14p (Paper presented at the New England Conference for Counseling and Development, 1987) (available from ERIC, No.ED299480)

Neely, Margery. Should We Whistle as We Shirk? What is Rape Prevention? 1985 20p (available from ERIC, No.ED262352)

Pritchard, Carol. Avoiding Rape On and Off Campus. Wenonah, NJ: State College Publishing Company, 1985

Proceedings of the National Conference on Rape Prevention Theory, Strategies, and Research, November 17-19, 1978. Columbus, OH: Women Against Rape, 1980

Rape: Prevention and Resistance. San Francisco: Queen's Bench Foundation, 1976

Rape: The First Sourcebook for Women. New York: New American Library, 1974

Reimold, Cheryl. The Women's Guide to Staying Safe. New York: Monarch Press, 1985

Rodabaugh, Barbara and Austin, Melanie. Sexual Assault: A Guide for Community Action. New York: Garland STPM Press, 1981

Sanford, Linda and Fetter, Ann. In Defense of Ourselves: A Rape Prevention Handbook for Women. Garden City, NY: Doubleday, 1979

Smith, Susan. Fear or Freedom: A Woman's Options in Social Survival and Physical Defense. Racine, WI: Mother Courage Press, 1986

Storaska, Frederic. How to Say No to a Rapist and Survive. New York: Random House, 1975

Stringer, Gayle and Rants-Rodriguez, Deanna. So What's It to Me? Sexual Assault Information for Guys. 1987 38p (available from ERIC, No.ED296243)

This is It!: Teen Acquaintance Rape Information and Prevention Activities for Groups. Seattle, WA: Alternatives to Fear, 1985

United States. Department of Health and Human Services. National Institute of Mental Health. Exemplary Rape Crisis Programs: A Cross-Site Analysis and Case Studies. Rockville, MD: The Department, 1985

_____. Rape and Older Women: A Guide to Prevention and Protection. Washington, DC: Government Printing Office, 1979

United States. Department of Justice. How to Protect Yourself Against Sexual Assault: Take a Bite Out of Crime. Washington, DC: Government Printing Office, 1979 16p

United States. Law Enforcement Assistance Administration. National Institute of Law Enforcement and Criminal Justice. Rape: Guidelines for a Community Response: An Executive Summary. Washington, DC: Government Printing Office, 1980 22p

Walker, Marcia and Brodsky, Stanley, eds. Sexual Assault: The Victim and the Rapist. Lexington, MA: Lexington Books, 1976

PREVENTION OF RAPE

ARTICLES

Amick, Angelynne and Calhoun, Karen. "Resistance to Sexual Aggression: Personality, Attitudinal, and Situational Factors", ARCHIVES OF SEXUAL BEHAVIOR 16(2):153-163 April 1987

Bart, P. and O'Brien, P. "Stopping Rape: Effective Avoidance Strategies", SIGNS 10:83-101 Autumn 1984

Bateman, Py. "Let's Get Out from between the Rock and Hard Place", JOURNAL OF INTERPERSONAL VIOLENCE 1(1):105-111 1986

Bell, Diane and Nelson, Topsy. "Speaking about Rape is Everyone's Business", WOMEN'S STUDIES INTERNATIONAL FORUM 12(4):403+ 1989

Block, Richard and Skogan, Wesley. "Resistance and Nonfatal Outcomes in Stranger-to-Stranger Predatory Crime", VIOLENCE AND VICTIMS 1(4):241-253 Winter 1986

Briskin, Karen and others. "Sexual Assault Programming for College Students", JOURNAL OF COUNSELING AND DEVELOPMENT 65(4):207-208 December 1986

Cohen, Pearl. "Resistance During Sexual Assaults: Avoiding Rape and Injury", VICTIMOLOGY 9(1):120-129 1984

Fischhoff, Baruch and others. "Rape Prevention: A Typology of Strategies", JOURNAL OF INTERPERSONAL VIOLENCE 2(3):292-308 1987

Furby, Lita and others. "Judged Effectiveness of Common Rape Prevention and Self-Defense Strategies", JOURNAL OF INTERPERSONAL VIOLENCE 4(1):44-64 March 1989

Graham, M. and others. "A Descriptive Study of Rape: 'Is Defensible Space a Solution?'", FREE INQUIRY IN CREATIVE SOCIOLOGY 14(2):173-176 November 1986

Gray, M. and others. "The Effectiveness of Personalizing Acquaintance Rape Prevention: Programs on Perception of Vulnerability and on Reducing Risk-Taking Behavior", JOURNAL OF COLLEGE STUDENT DEVELOPMENT 31(3):217-220 May 1990

Hazelwood, R. and Harpold, J. "Rape: The Dangers of Providing Confrontational Advice", FBI LAW ENFORCEMENT BULLETIN 55:1-5 June 1986

Krulewitz, J. and Kahn, A. "Preferences for Rape Reduction Strategies", PSYCHOLOGY OF WOMEN QUARTERLY 7:301-312 Summer 1983

Lee, Lucienne. "Rape Prevention: Experiential Training for Men", JOURNAL OF COUNSELING AND DEVELOPMENT 66(2):100-101 October 1987

Leland-Young, Jan and Nelson, Joan. "Prevention of Sexual Assault through the Resocialization of Women: Unlearning Victim Behavior", WOMEN AND THERAPY 6(1):203-210 Spring/Summer 1987

"Putting an End to Military Rape", WOMEN IN ACTION 3:3+ October 1988

Quinsey, Vernon and Upfold, Douglas. "Rape Completion and Victim Injury as a Function of Female Resistance Strategy", CANADIAN JOURNAL OF BEHAVIORAL SCIENCES 17(1):40-50 January 1985

Ruback, R. and Ivie, Deborah. "Prior Relationship, Resistance, and Injury in Rapes: An Analysis of Crisis Center Reports", VIOLENCE AND VICTIMS 3(2):99-111 Summer 1988

Siegel, J. and others. "Resistance to Sexual Assault: Who Resists and What Happens?", AMERICAN JOURNAL OF PUBLIC HEALTH 79:27-31 January 1989

Torrey, Sally and Lee, Ruth. "Curbing Date Violence: Campus-Wide Strategies", JOURNAL OF THE NATIONAL ASSOCIATION OF WOMEN DEANS, ADMINISTRATORS, AND COUNSELORS 51(1):3-8 Fall 1987

Underwood, M. and Fiedler, N. "The Crisis of Rape: A Community Response", COMMUNITY MENTAL HEALTH JOURNAL 19:227-230 Fall 1983

Youn, Gahyun. "On Using Public Media for Prevention of Rape", PSYCHOLOGICAL REPORTS 61:237-238 August 1987

LEGAL ISSUES

BOOKS, DOCUMENTS, PAMPHLETS

Estrich, Susan. Real Rape: How the Legal System Victimizes Women Who Say No. London: Harvard University Press, 1987

Feild, Hubert and Biemen, Leigh. Jurors and Rape: A Study in Psychology and Law. Lexington, MA: Lexington Books, 1980

Gill, Wanda. Gender Bias in the Courts. 1987 20p (available from ERIC, No.ED288808)

Green, William. Rape: The Evidential Examination and Management of the Adult Female Victim. Lexington, MA: Lexington Books, 1988

LaFree, Gary. Rape and Criminal Justice: The Social Construction of Sexual Assault. Belmont, CA: Wadsworth Publishing, 1989

MacKinnon, Catharine. Feminism Unmodified: Discourse on Life and Law. Cambridge, MA: Harvard University Press, 1987

Rodabaugh, Barbara and Austin, Melanie. Sexual Assault: A Guide for Community Action. New York: Garland STPM Press, 1981

Tong, Rosemary. Women, Sex and the Law. Totawa, NJ: Rowman and Allanheld, 1984

United States. Congress. House. Committee on the Judiciary. Sexual Abuse Act of 1986: Hearing. Washington, DC: Government Printing Office, 1986 91p

_____. Sexual Abuse Act of 1986: Report. Washington, DC: Government Printing Office, 1986 30p

United States. Congress. Senate. Committee on the Judiciary. Impact of Media Coverage of Rape Trials: Hearing. Washington, DC: Government Printing Office, 1985 99p

LEGAL ISSUES

ARTICLES

Adler, Z. "The Relevance of Sexual History Evidence in Rape: Problems of Subjective Interpretation", THE CRIMINAL LAW REVIEW December 1985, p769-780

"The Admissibility of Expert Testimony on Rape Trauma Syndrome", JOURNAL OF CRIMINAL LAW AND CRIMINOLOGY 75:1366-1416 Winter 1984

Brekke, N and Borgida, E. "Expert Psychological Testimony in Rape Trials: A Social-Cognitive Analysis", JOURNAL OF PERSONALITY AND SOCIAL PSYCHOLOGY 55:372-386 September 1988

Bristow, Ann. "State v. Masks: An Analysis of Expert Testimony on Rape Trauma Syndrome", VICTIMOLOGY 9(2):273-281 1984

Buchele, B. and Buchele, J. "Legal and Psychological Issues in the Use of Expert Testimony on Rape Trauma Syndrome", WASHBURN LAW JOURNAL 25:26-42 Fall 1985

Bumiller, Kristin. "Rape as a Legal Symbol: An Essay on Sexual Violence and Racism", UNIVERSITY OF MIAMI LAW REVIEW 42(1):75-91 September 1987

Caringella-MacDonald, Susan. "The Comparability in Sexual And Nonsexual Assault Case Treatment: Did Statute Change Meet the Objective?", CRIME AND DELINQUENCY 31(2):206-222 April 1985

_____. "Marxist and Feminist Interpretations on the Aftermath of Rape Reforms", CONTEMPORARY CRISES 12(2):125-143 June 1988

_____. "Parallels and Pitfalls: The Aftermath of Legal Reform for Sexual Assault, Marital Rape, and Domestic Violence Victims", JOURNAL OF INTERPERSONAL VIOLENCE 3(2):147-189 June 1988

_____. "Sexual Assault Prosecution: An Examination of Model Rape Legislation in Michigan", WOMEN AND POLITICS 4(3):65-82 Fall 1984

"Checking the Allure of Increased Conviction Rates: The Admissibility of Expert Testimony on Rape Trauma Syndrome in Criminal Proceedings", VIRGINIA LAW REVIEW 70:1657-1705 November 1984

Cling, B. "Rape Trauma Syndrome: Medical Evidence of Non-Consent", WOMEN'S RIGHTS LAW REPORTER 10(4):243-259 Fall 1988

_____. "Rape Trauma Syndrome: Medical Evidence of Non-Consent", MEDICAL TRIAL TECHNIQUE QUARTERLY 35:154-181 Winter 1988

"The Constitutionality of an Absolute Privilege for Rape Crisis Counseling: A Criminal Defendant's Sixth Amendment Rights Versus a Rape Victim's Right to Confidential Therapeutic Counseling", BOSTON COLLEGE LAW REVIEW 30:411-476 March 1989

"The Constitutionality of Statutorily Restricting Public Access to Judicial Proceedings: The Case of the Rape Shield Mandatory Closure Provision", BOSTON UNIVERSITY LAW REVIEW 66:271-310 March 1986

Coombs, Mary. "Crime in the Stacks, or a Tale of a Text: A Feminist Response to a Criminal Law Textbook", JOURNAL OF LEGAL EDUCATION 38(1/2):117-135 March/June 1988

"Criminal Law: Kansas Recognizes Rape Trauma Syndrome", WASHBURN LAW JOURNAL 24:653-665 Spring 1985

"Culpable Mistakes in Rape: Eliminating the Defense of Unreasonable Mistake of Fact as to Victim Consent", DICKINSON LAW REVIEW 89:473-499 Winter 1985

Davis, Elizabeth. "Rape Shield Statutes: Legislative Responses to Probative Dangers", WASHINGTON UNIVERSITY JOURNAL OF URBAN AND CONTEMPORARY LAW 27:271-294 1984

"Distinguishing Rape: A Definitive Approach to Sexual Assault", VERMONT LAW REVIEW 10:353-381 Fall 1985

Estrich, Susan. "Rape", THE YALE LAW JOURNAL 95(6):1087-1184 May 1986

"Expert Testimony on Rape Trauma Syndrome: An Argument for Limited Admissibility", WASHINGTON LAW REVIEW 63:1063-1086 October 1988

"The Footprints of Fear: Prosecution Use of Expert Testimony on the Rape Trauma Syndrome", WAYNE LAW REVIEW 33:179-203 Fall 1986

Fraizer, Patricia and Borgida, Eugene. "Rape Trauma Syndrome Evidence in Court", AMERICAN PSYCHOLOGIST 40(9):984-993 September 1985

Frossard, M. "When the Accuser Recants: People v. Dotson", LITIGATION 14:11-16+ Summer 1988

Galvin, H. "Shielding Rape Victims in the State and Federal Courts: A Proposal for the Second Decade", MINNESOTA LAW REVIEW 70:763-916 April 1986

Giacopassi, David and Wilkinson, Karen. "Rape and the Devalued Victim", LAW AND HUMAN BEHAVIOR 9(4):367-383 December 1985

Graham, Ernest. "Rape Trauma Syndrome: Is It Probative of Lack of Consent?", LAW AND PSYCHOLOGY REVIEW 13:25-42 Spring 1989

Griffiths, G. "Psychological Factors: The Overlooked Evidence in Rape Investigations", FBI LAW ENFORCEMENT BULLETIN 54:8-15 April 1985

Heilbrun, Alfred, Jr. and Heilbrun, Mark. "The Treatment of Women within the Criminal Justice System: An Inquiry into the Social Impact of the Women's Rights Movement", PSYCHOLOGY OF WOMEN QUARTERLY 10(3):240-251 September 1986

Holtzman, Elizabeth. "Women and the Law", VILLANOVA LAW REVIEW 31(5):1429-1438 September 1986

"Identifying the Rape Victim: A Constitutional Clash between the First Amendment and the Right to Privacy", JOHN MARSHALL LAW REVIEW 18:987-1014 Summer 1985

Kanin, E. and others. "Personal Sexual History and Punitive Judgments for Rape", PSYCHOLOGICAL REPORTS 61:439-442 October 1987

Katz, S. "Expectation and Desire in the Law of Forcible Rape", SAN DIEGO LAW REVIEW 26:21-71 January 1989

Kelly, D. "Delivering Legal Services to Victims: An Evaluation and Prescription", THE JUSTICE SYSTEM JOURNAL 9:62-86 Spring 1984

Kidd, Kathryn. "Rape Legislation as Social Policy: Changing Policy, Changing Laws", FREE INQUIRY IN CREATIVE SOCIOLOGY 15(2):169-173 November 1987

LaFree, Gary and others. "Jurors' Responses to Victims' Behavior and Legal Issues in Sexual Assault Trials", SOCIAL PROBLEMS 32(4):389-407 April 1985

Lauderdale, H. "The Admissibility of Expert Testimony on Rape Trauma Syndrome", JOURNAL OF CRIMINAL LAW AND CRIMINOLOGY 75:1366-1416 Winter 1984

LeBeau, James. "Statute Revision and the Reporting of Rape [California]", SOCIOLOGY AND SOCIAL RESEARCH 72(3):201-207 April 1988

Loggans, S. "Rape as an Intentional Tort", TRIAL 21:45-48+ October 1985

MacKinnon, Catherine. "Feminism, Marxism, Method, and the State: Toward Feminist Jurisprudence", SIGNS 8(4):635-658 Summer 1983

Marshall, W. and Barbaree, H. "A Behavioral View of Rape", INTERNATIONAL JOURNAL OF LAW AND PSYCHIATRY 7:51-77 1984

Massaro, T. "Experts, Psychology, Credibility, and Rape: The Rape Trauma Syndrome Issue and Its Implications for Expert Psychological Testimony", MINNESOTA LAW REVIEW 69:395-470 February 1985

McCord, D. "The Admissibility of Expert Testimony Regarding Rape Trauma Syndrome in Rape Prosecutions", BOSTON COLLEGE LAW REVIEW 26:1143-1213 September 1985

Nelligan, Peter. "The Effects of the Gender of Jurors on Sexual Assault Verdicts", SOCIOLOGY AND SOCIAL RESEARCH 72(4):249-251 July 1988

Nemeth, C. "Legal Emancipation for the Victim of Rape", HUMAN RIGHTS 11:30-35 Winter 1984

Neuhauser, Maxine. "The Privilege of Confidentiality and Rape Crisis Counselors", WOMEN'S RIGHTS LAW REPORTER 8(3):185-196 Summer 1985

Olsen, F. "Statutory Rape: A Feminist Critique of Rights Analysis", TEXAS LAW REVIEW 63:387-432 November 1984

Omolade, B. "Black Women, Black Men, and Tawana Brawley -- The Shared Condition", HARVARD WOMEN'S LAW JOURNAL 12:11-23 Spring 1989

Pineau, L. "Date Rape: A Feminist Analysis", LAW AND PHILOSOPHY 8:217-243 August 1989

Pitch, T. "Critical Criminology, the Construction of Social Problems, and the Question of Rape", INTERNATIONAL JOURNAL OF THE SOCIOLOGY THE LAW 13:35-46 February 1985

"Protecting Rape Victims from Civil Suits by Their Attackers", LAW AND INEQUALITY 8:279-308 November 1989

"Rape: Adding Insult to Injury", VERMONT LAW REVIEW 11:361-372 Spring 1986

"Rape Shield Laws -- Is It Time for Reinforcement?", UNIVERSITY OF MICHIGAN JOURNAL OF LAW REFORM 21:317-345 Fall 1987/Winter 1988

"Rape Shield Statutes: Constitutional Despite Unconstitutional Exclusions of Evidence", WISCONSIN LAW REVIEW 1985, p1219-1272

"Rape Shield Statutes: Legislative Responses to Probative Dangers", WASHINGTON UNIVERSITY JOURNAL OF URBAN AND CONTEMPORARY LAW 27:271-294 1984

"Rape Trauma Syndrome", HARVARD WOMEN'S LAW JOURNAL 7:301-308 Spring 1984

"Rape Trauma Syndrome", MISSOURI LAW REVIEW 50:945-967 Fall 1985

"'Rape Trauma Syndrome' and Inconsistent Rulings on Its Admissibility around the Nation", WILLAMETTE LAW REVIEW 24:1011-1034 Fall 1988

"Rape Trauma Syndrome: Interest of the Victim and Neutral Experts", UNIVERSITY OF CHICAGO LEGAL FORUM 1989, p399-420

"Rape Victim Confrontation", UTAH LAW REVIEW 1985, p687-722

"Rape Victim-Crisis Counselor Communications: An Argument for an Absolute Privilege", U.C. DAVIS LAW REVIEW 17:1213-1245 Summer 1984

Resick, P. "Psychological Effects of Victimization: Implications for the Criminal Justice System", CRIME AND DELINQUENCY 33:468-478 October 1987

_____. "The Trauma of Rape and the Criminal Justice System", JUSTICE SYSTEM JOURNAL 9:52-61 Spring 1984

Sahjpaul, S. and Renner, K. "The New Sexual Assault Law: The Victim's Experience in Court", AMERICAN JOURNAL OF COMMUNITY PSYCHOLOGY 16:503-513 August 1988

Schafran, Lynn. "Documenting Gender Bias in the Courts: The Task Force Approach", JUDICATURE 70(5):280-290 February/March 1987

Searles, Patricia and Berger, Ronald. "The Current Status of Rape Reform Legislation: An Examination of State Statutes", WOMEN'S RIGHTS LAW REPORTER 10(1):25-43 Spring 1987

Snider, Laureen. "Legal Reform and Social Control: The Dangers of Abolishing Rape", INTERNATIONAL JOURNAL OF THE SOCIOLOGY OF LAW 13(4):337-356 November 1985

Soshnick, A. "The Rape Shield Paradox: Complainant Protection Amidst Oscillating Trends of State Judicial Interpretation", JOURNAL OF CRIMINAL LAW AND CRIMINOLOGY 78:644-698 Fall 1987

Steffensmeier, Darrell. "The Uniqueness of Rape? Disposition and Sentencing Outcomes of Rape in Comparison to Other Major Felonies", SOCIOLOGY AND SOCIAL RESEARCH 72(3):192-198 April 1988

Steketee, G. and Austin, A. "Rape Victims and the Justice System: Utilization and Impact", SOCIAL SERVICE REVIEW 63:285-303 June 1989

Taylor, Julie. "Rape and Women's Credibility: Problems of Recantations and False Accusations Echoed in the Case of Cathleen Crowell Webb and Gary Dotson", HARVARD WOMEN'S LAW JOURNAL 10:59-116 Spring 1987

Tchen, C. "Rape Reform and a Statutory Consent Defense", JOURNAL OF CRIMINAL LAW AND CRIMINOLOGY 74:1518-1555 Winter 1983

Temkin, J. "Regulating Sexual History Evidence -- The Limits of Discretionary Legislation", INTERNATIONAL AND COMPARATIVE LAW QUARTERLY 33:942-978 October 1984

Tetreault, Patricia. "Rape Myth Acceptance: A Case for Providing Educational Expert Testimony in Rape Jury Trials", BEHAVIORAL SCIENCES AND THE LAW 7(2):243-257 Spring 1989

"The Use of Rape Trauma Syndrome as Evidence in a Rape Trial: Valid or Invalid?", WAKE FOREST LAW REVIEW 21:93-120 Spring 1985

"The Use of Scientific Evidence in Rape Prosecutions", UNIVERSITY OF RICHMOND LAW REVIEW 18:851-873 Summer 1984

Walsh, A. "Placebo Justice: Victim Recommendations and Offender Sentences in Sexual Assault Cases", JOURNAL OF CRIMINAL LAW AND CRIMINOLOGY 77:1126-1141 Winter 1986

West, L. "Is Saying 'No' Enough?", THE MARYLAND BAR JOURNAL 20:8-13 March 1987

Wiener, Richard and Grisso, T. "Empathy and Biased Assimilation of Testimonies in Cases of Alleged Rape", LAW AND HUMAN BEHAVIOR 13:343-355 December 1989

_____ **and Vodanovich, Stephen.** "The Evaluation of Culpability for Rape: A Model of Legal Decision Making", JOURNAL OF PSYCHOLOGY 120(5):489-500 September 1986

RESOURCES

STATISTICS

Cameron, Paul and others. Is the Rape Rate Increasing? 1987 13p (Paper presented at the Eastern Psychological Association, 1987) (available from ERIC, No.ED293015)

Jaffee, D. and Straus, M. "Sexual Climate and Reported Rape: A State-Level Analysis", ARCHIVES OF SEXUAL BEHAVIOR 16:107-123 April 1987

Koss, M. "The Scope of Rape: Incidence and Prevalence of Sexual Aggression and Victimization in a National Sample of Higher Education Students", JOURNAL OF CONSULTING AND CLINICAL PSYCHOLOGY 55(2):162-170 April 1987

_____ **and others**. Hidden Rape: Incidence and Prevalence of Sexual Aggression and Victimization in a National Sample of Students in Higher Education. 1985 31p (Research sponsored by United States, Department of Health and Human Services, National Center for the Control and Prevention of Rape) (available from ERIC, No.ED267321)

LeBeau, J. "Patterns of Stranger and Serial Rape Offending: Factors Distinguishing Apprehended and at Large Offenders", JOURNAL OF CRIMINAL LAW AND CRIMINOLOGY 78:309-326 Summer 1987

Russell, Diana. "The Prevalence and Incidence of Forcible Rape and Attempted Rape of Females", VICTIMOLOGY 7(1/4):81-93 1982

United States. Department of Justice. Federal Bureau of Investigation. Age-Specific Arrest Rates and Race Specific Arrest Rates for Selected Offenses, 1965-1987. Washington, DC: The Bureau (annual)

_____ . Population-at-Risk Rates and Selected Crime Indicators. Washington, DC: The Bureau (annual) (section on forcible rape)

_____ . Uniform Crime Reports: Crime in the U.S. Washington, DC: Government Printing Office (annual)

United States. Department of Justice. Office of Justice Programs. Criminal Victimization, 1987. Washington, DC: Government Printing Office, 1988 6p (Bureau of Justice Statistics Bulletin) (annual)

_____ . Households Touched by Crime, 1988. Washington, DC: Government Printing Office, 1989 6p (Bureau of Justice Statistics Bulletin)

_____ . International Crime Rates. Washington, DC: Government Printing Office, 1988 11p (Bureau of Justice Statistics Special Reports)

_____ . Prosecution of Felony Arrests. Washington, DC: Government Printing Office (annual)

_____ . Report to the Nation on Crime and Justice. Washington, DC: Government Printing Office, 1988

_____ . Seasonality of Crime Victimization. Washington, DC: Government Printing Office, 1988 12p (National Crime Survey)

_____. Sentencing Outcomes in 28 Felony Courts, 1985. Washington, DC: Government Printing Office, 1985 41p

_____. Sourcebook of Criminal Justice Statistics. Washington, DC: Government Printing Office (annual)

_____. Violent Crime Trends. Washington, DC: Government Printing Office, 1987 6p (Bureau of Justice Statistics Special Reports)

United States. **Department of Justice. Bureau of Justice Statistics.** The Crime of Rape. Washington, DC: The Department, 1985 7p

_____. International Crime Rates. Washington, DC: The Department, 1988 13p (compares crime rates, including rape, in the European countries, Canada, Australia, New Zealand and the United States)

United States. **Department of Justice. National Criminal Justice Information and Statistics Service.** Rape Victimization in 26 American Cities. Washington, DC: Government Printing Office, 1979 67p

BIBLIOGRAPIES

Barnes, Dorothy. Rape, a Bibliography, 1965-1975. Troy, NY: Whitston Publishing, 1977

Bibliographic Guide to the Files of the National Clearinghouse on Marital Rape. [n.p.] 1981 (located in the Marital Rape Collection, University of Illinois at Urbana-Champaign)

Brodsky, Stanley. Sexual Assault: An Annotated Bibliography and Literature Review. Cambridge, England: Institute of Criminology, 1979

Evans, Hannah and Sperekas, Nicole. Sexual Assault Bibliography, 1920-1975. Washington: American Psychological Association, 1976

Gehr, Marilyn. Women as Victims of Violence: Battered Wives/Rape: A Selected Annotated Bibliography. Albany: State University of New York, 1978

Gibbons, Don. "Forcible Rape: Current Knowledge and Research Issues", CRIMINAL JUSTICE ABSTRACTS 15(1):100-112 March 1983

Kemmer, Elizabeth. Rape and Rape-Related Issues: An Annotated Bibliography. New York: Garland Publications, 1977

LeGrand, Camille. Institutional Liability for Sexual Assault: An Annotated Bibliography of Selected Legal Cases. San Francisco: Institute for the Prevention and Control of Rape, 1984

Lystad, Mary. "Sexual Abuse in the Home: A Review of the Literature", INTERNATIONAL JOURNAL OF FAMILY PSYCHIATRY 3(1):3-31 1982

Men and Sexuality: Bibliography of Selected Resources. New York: Planned Parenthood Federation of America, 1985 11p

Phillips, Dretha. Social Policy and the Legal Response to Rape: A Bibliography with Selected Annotations. Monticello, IL: Vance Bibliographies, 1983

70

Rape Bibliography. Washington, DC: Center for Women Policy Studies, 1974

United States. Department of Justice. National Institute for Law Enforcement and Criminal Justice. Forcible Rape: A Literature Review and Annotated Bibliography. Washington, DC: Government Printing Office, 1978

Weiner, Neil and Pastor, Selma. Bibliography of Bibliographies on Criminal Violence. Philadelphia, PA: Center for Studies in Criminology and Criminal Law, University of Pennsylvania, 1984

White, Anthony. Rape: An Urban Crime?: A Selected Bibliography. Monticello, IL: Council of Planning Librarians, 1977 15p

DIRECTORIES

Center for Women Policy Studies. Sexual Assault. Washington, DC: The Center [n.d.] (resource collection, includes material on marital rape)

Marital Rape Information Collection, University of Illinois at Urbana-Champaign, Library (a collection of articles and newspaper clippings about marital rape) (access through the Women's Studies Reading Room)

National Center on Women and Family Law. Marital Rape Exemption Packet. New York: The Center [n.d.] (state by state summary of the marital rape exemption in state criminal statutes, a bibliography of legal articles on marital rape)

United States. Department of Health and Human Services. Centers for Disease Control. Rape Prevention and Services to Rape Victims. Atlanta, GA: The Department, 1982

United States. Department of Health and Human Services. National Institute of Mental Health. National Directory: Rape Prevention and Treatment Resources. Washington, DC: Government Printing Office, 1981

United States. Department of Health, Education, and Welfare. National Institute of Mental Health. National Center for the Prevention and Control of Rape. Materials Available from the National Rape Information Clearinghouse. Rockville, MD: The Department, 1979

Webster, Linda, ed. Sexual Assault and Child Sexual Abuse: A National Directory of Victim Services and Prevention Programs. Phoenix, AZ: Oryx Press, 1989

ORGANIZATIONS

ENDING MEN'S VIOLENCE TASK GROUP, National Organization for Changing Men, Box 93, Charleston, IL 61920

FEMINIST ALLIANCE AGAINST RAPE, P.O. Box 21033, Washington, DC 20009

NATIONAL CENTER ON WOMEN AND FAMILY LAW, 799 Broadway, Room 402, New York, NY 10003

NATIONAL COALITION AGAINST SEXUAL ASSAULT, 2428 Ontario Road, NW, Washington, DC 20009

NATIONAL VICTIM CENTER, 307 West 7th Street, Suite 1001, Fort Worth, TX 76102

PEOPLE AGAINST RAPE, P.O. Box 160, Chicago, IL 60635

PEOPLE ORGANIZED TO STOP RAPE OF IMPRISONED PERSONS, P.O. Box 632, Fort Bragg, CA 95437